T0288363

HOW THE LIGHT GETS IN

Books & Chapbooks by Kirk Robertson

The Burning Fire Chief (1975)
Shooting At Shadows Killing Crows (1975)
Drinking Beer At 22 Below (1976)
Two Weeks Off (1977, 1984)
Walked On By 40 Camels (1977)
Sultry Afternoon With The Blinds Partly Pulled (1978)
Shovel Off To Buffalo (1978)
Under The Weight Of The Sky (1978)
Coffee Dust Devils & Old Rodeo Bulls (1979)
High Fallon Southern Comfort (1980)
Nevada (1980)
Origins Initiations (1980)
Reasons And Methods (1981)
West Nevada Waltz (1981)
art•i•facts (1985)
Matters Of Equal Height (1987)
Driving To Vegas: New & Selected Poems 1969-1987 (1989)
Music: A Suite & 13 Songs (1995)
Just Past Labor Day: New & Selected Poems 1969-1995 (1996)
Shoes (with Valería de Serpa) (1997)
How The Light Gets In:
New & Collected Poems 1969-2014 (2014)

How the Light Gets In

New and Collected Poems 1969–2014

Kirk Robertson

Rainshadow Editions
The Black Rock Press
University of Nevada, Reno
2014

ISBN 978-1-891033-69-8
Library of Congress Control Number: 2014939251
Printed in the United States of America

The Black Rock Press
University of Nevada, Reno
Reno, NV 89557-0224
www.blackrockpress.org

The publication of this book was supported by a generous grant from the Nell J. Redfield Foundation.

Cover Image

Joseph Cornell, Untitled *(First Collage in a Long Time)*, collage with pencil on masonite, 11.875 x 8.875 inches, 1959. Collection of Robert Lehrman, courtesy of Aimee and Robert Lehrman, © the Joseph and Robert Cornell Memorial Foundation, licensed by VAGA, New York, NY. Photograph by Mark Gulezian/Quicksilver.

Frontispiece

Joseph Cornell, *Toward the Blue Peninsula (for Emily Dickinson)*, box construction, 14.5 x 10.25 x 5.5 inches, c. 1953. The Robert Lehrman Art Trust, courtesy of Aimee and Robert Lehrman, © the Joseph and Robert Cornell Memorial Foundation, licensed by VAGA, New York, NY. Photograph by Mark Gulezian/Quicksilver.

for Valerie and Valería

CONTENTS

Fahrenheit 451 At 22 Below

Shooting At Shadows Killing Crows

Under The Weight Of The Sky

Origins Initiations

Reasons And Methods

No Deposit No Return

Hindsight

West Nevada Waltz

PAINTING

DRIVING TO VEGAS

Music

Just Past Labor Day

ACKNOWLEDGMENTS

I'd like to especially thank Bob Blesse for his commitment to seeing this book in print.

The drawings in the *Matters of Equal Height* section are based on pictographs from an Iroquois mnemonic cane.

The drawings accompanying the poems in *Two Weeks Off* are by David Barker.

The poems in the section *Shoes* were written in collaboration with Valería de Serpa.

Thanks are also due to the editors/publishers of the following broadsides, magazines, anthologies, chapbooks and books where earlier versions of some of these poems first appeared.

A, Abraxas, American Freeway: Best Of American Small Press Poets (Maro Verlag), *The American Literary Review, American Poets Say Goodbye To The Twentieth Century* (Four Walls, Eight Windows), *The Americas Anthology* (New Rivers), *Amorotica: New Erotic Poetry* (Deep River), *Arts Alive, Benzene, Blackjack, The Burning Fire Chief* (Wormwood Review), *Cafe Solo, Cenizas: Literature & Art, Cloudline, Coffee Dust Devils and Old Rodeo Bulls* (Judson Crews), *Cold Drill, The Coldsprings Journal, Contemporary Quarterly, Correspondence Art* (Visual Arts Press), *Coyote's Journal, Crawlspace, Desert Wood: An Anthology Of Nevada Poets* (University of Nevada), *Drinking Beer at 22 Below* (Nausea Press), *Driving to*

Vegas: New & Selected Poems 1969-1987 (Sun/Gemini), *The Echo, Et Cetera, Fireweed, Five Card Stud: Five Contemporary Poets* (Duck Down), *Floating Island, Gasolin, A Geography Of Poets* (Bantam), *Great Basin News, The Greenfield Review, High Country News, High Desert Journal, High Fallon Southern Comfort* (Maelstrom Press), *Home Planet News, House Organ, Hyperion, Idaho Arts Journal, Indian Poems* (Luna Bisonte Prods), *In Focus, Intermedia, Interstate, Invisible City, Italia America, Just Past Labor Day: Selected and New Poems 1969-1995* (University of Nevada), *Kaldron, Kangaroo Court, Kudzu, The Lahontan Valley News, The Limberlost Review, Literary Nevada* (University of Nevada Press), *A Long Line Of Joy* (Big Boulevard), *Madrona, Matters of Equal Height* (West Coast Poetry Review), *The McLean County Poetry Review, The Meadows, Men Talk* (Deep River Press), *Mojo Navigator(e), Music: A Suite & 13 Songs* (Floating Island), *neon, Nevada* (Road House Press), *Nevada Magazine, The Nevada Poet: An Anthology* (A Frosty Morning Press), *The Nevada Weekly, New Directions, A New Geography Of Poets* (University of Arkansas), *New Work(s)* (Duck Down), *Nexus, O.Ars, Offerta Speciale, Olympia, On The Bus, Open Ring, The Orchard, Origins Initiations* (Turkey Press), *Oro Madre, Orpheus, The Pikestaff Forum, PinchPenny, Poemelon, Poetry NOW, Poetry Of The American Indian* (American Visual Communication), *Purr, Reasons and Methods* (Rainbow Resin), *Reno Gazette Journal, road/house, Rocky Mountain Creative Arts Journal, Scree, Selected Tumblewords* (University of Nevada), *Seven Nevada Poets* (Rainshadow Editions), *Shoes* (Black Rock Press), *Shooting at Shadows Killing Crows* (Blue Cloud Quarterly), *Shovel Off to Buffalo* (Wormwood Review), *616 Center 1, The Smudge, Snowy Egret, South Dakota Review, The Stoogism Anthology* (Scarecrow Press), *Street, Sultry Afternoon With the Blinds Partly Pulled* (Lion's Breath Press), *Swamp Root, Sweet Little Sixteen, Talisman, Telephone, Terpentin On The Rocks:*

Poems From The Small Presses Of The U.S. (Maro Verlag), *Thorn Apple, TumbleWords: Writers Rolling Around The West (*University of Nevada), *Two Weeks Off* (Floating Island), *Under the Weight of the Sky* (Cherry Valley Editions), *Uzzano, Vagabond, The Vagabond Anthology, Walked on by 40 Camels* (Rocky Mountain Creative Arts Journal), *Wanbli Ho, West Conscious Review, West Nevada Waltz* (Turkey Press), *Whetstone, Wind, Wine Rings, The Wormwood Review, Yard Sale (*Bunchgrass Press), *Yellow Brick Road* and *100 Mesotics for John Cage* (College of Creative Studies, UCSB).

FAHRENHEIT 451 AT 22 BELOW

if your urn is sufficiently Grecian
it will ofttimes get away
with being a crock of shit

—Gerald Locklin

to do a dull thing with style
is preferable to doing a dangerous thing
without it

—Charles Bukowski

Windfall

Twisted gnarled
wood below he sat
yearning over the edge

Wheat Field With Crows, 1890

He played in
the orchestra
first violin

Second row
never much
considered

Reincarnation
before attending
LACMA's Van

Gogh retrospective
lines extended
around the block

It was hot 102°
and smoggy he
felt a certain

Ringing in his
ears when he saw
a priest walk

Down the street
disappear around
the turn of the century

Halloween

Eyes feel like triangles
cut with a kitchen

Knife removed on a
day in October it's

Difficult to speak of
anything everything

Slopes down in every
direction dancing like

A Halloween masque
of pregnant pumpkins

George C. Scott would
love to devour whole

Cracking the seeds
on his canines

Brontosaurus Blues

Muddy's blues a wet
emulsion rain streaked
windows distant trees

Drinking wine pushing
smoke zeroes out hoping
they add up to something

More the only thing that's
closer is tomorrow it's
skinnier everyday *sail on*

My little honey bee sail on
just listen to that harp
humming along like a

Tipped over brontosaurus
I don't mind you sailin' but
puleeze don't you sail so long

Small Ritual For J.K.

nowhere to go but everywhere
so just keep rolling under the stars
—Jack Kerouac

Heard the news a day or
two ago beer and a shot
at the Railroad Room then

On down to the tracks in
the old Westwood millyard
watch the moon come up

Over the ridge marvel at the
clear starry night listen to
howl of that ole desolation

Angel coyote up at the end
of some lonesome long
forgotten high sierra road

The Clorox Kid

He scrubbed the floor
occasionally got called
on these jobs someone

Dying got to be too
much of a mess and it
had to be disposed of

He was resting up for
the nightly nine o'clock
cardiac crapout coupled

With overdoses on this
and that when they
wheeled in this kid who'd

Drunk clorox wishing
it was sweet wine not
just a sip or two but a

Whole half gallon when
he got there to mop up
the entire ward smelled

Like clorox his liver
was gone the doctor
too nothing to do

Nothing that could be
done the kid sterilized
the room simply by

Dying in it he punched
out at eleven in the
morning the kid was

Cut into small squares
they scoured the walls
the sinks the floors

With him punching in
the next day even the
time clock exuded a

Soft clorox hum as
he dipped the mop in
and started scrubbing

Love Poems

Like the late
worm usually

Miss the bird
entirely

Election Night

He comes in the door fifth
of Wild Turkey ready to
celebrate two hours before

The polls close talks about
the new job he'll soon have
depending of course on the

Outcome is particularly
concerned about how I
voted says I should support

And participate in the
greatest system ever
set up the one Columbus

Brought over Jefferson
wrote down moved west
to wipe out the buffalo

Put him in line for a thirty
nine grand a year job with
the BIA it all depends on

Pennsylvania he says then
we'll know but something
about him doesn't sit right

Growls and snaps as
Columbus must have
thankful for land at last

But knowing neither
where he's landed
nor where he's at

5:30 News

They ask the winos
if they're worried

I think it's a woman
she dresses like a man

I don't sleep out
no more you betcha

You only gotta die once
God takes care of me

They ask the police
if there are clues the

Police are worried
they only know

It's a person who
carries a knife they

Ask the winos if
they're worried

About the future
What future?

Seven dead throats
slashed in six weeks

The Slasher loose
on CBS news

Arlee

Wide spot on pray for
me I drive Highway 93
diesel smoke hangs in

Frigid gray November
air xmas lights droop in
frosted store windows

Stepping out of the Evaro
Bar to blood thick in the
pickup bed spilling from

The gutted eyes of a five
point buck staring up
into drifting snow he

Shuddered suddenly in the
cold blood quickly freezes
to ice at twenty below

Owl

He got there first let
himself in they came
home later asked if he

Saw owl on the roof
last time we saw that
someone died maybe

You should stay over
he agreed to stay but
they left first thing next

Morning before the phone
rang a friend of theirs
a miscarriage they said

But she wasn't pregnant
what can we do he asks
just tell them she says

Hangs up maybe owl
was for her or maybe
for the miscarried one

Who was not conceived
but had something to say
and no way to do it he

Thought maybe that's
what he stayed an extra
day to hear maybe it's

Why they put canaries
in coal mines

The Mighty Hunter

Keeps at least one loaded
gun in car shop and house
just in case shoots at every

Thing that moves a lot of
what doesn't can hit two
dimes in the air with a

Single shot .22 runs over
one afternoon to ask if
anyone wants a pet crow

Cuz he's just dropped one
somewhere out in the road
claims prowess as a hunter

From his indian heritage
but something's gone awry
his instincts and those of

The animals he claims relation
to crossed like hairs in the
scope they no longer seem to

Understand one another he
wonders where all the jack
rabbits have gone why when

Someone's dog gets shot
they always think he did it

A Discussion Concerning Lodging

He's the big indian trader
an ex-smoker you should
have seen it he says

The car was bent double
she'd been cut in half
dead instantly the guy

With her so drunk he's
sitting on her asking
for cigarettes an old lady

Walks in with something
to sell I know you're indian
she says you give me same

When I'm drunk when
I'm sober as she leaves
he looks back at me

At my cigarette and
says *your* rent is due

Sunday Service At Short Bear's House

He was bundled up
sent off to meet his
his father the preacher

In the church barely
twenty yards from
the house he wasn't

Missed until his father
returned after evening
services they searched

Everywhere all day
into the next found
nothing until Goose

Found him four or five
miles northeast of the
church frozen dead

Just a little ways from
Short Bear's house
I thought I heard

Coyote crying ten
o'clock Sunday night
Short Bear said

A Letter To Boston

to bring in food, fresh meat
running blood down work
& laugh twisted faces
—Stuart Z. Perkoff

You write of Mandan
and buffalo both of
which are almost gone

I sit here try to write
between indians at
the door thinking I'm

Connected with the
trading post to hock
their radios rifles and

Tape decks numerous as
buffalo were once fresh
meat for laugh twisted faces

Almost as numerous as
coyote's wine bottles that
fill the empty lot in town

A glistening green-white
dance shards for some
future archaeological dig

Top Pieces For The Axis Nave

—a found poem

Please untie
the wheels
of your car

And respectively
put one top
piece through

The middle
hole of the rim
then mount

The wheels
again tighten
as usually

Then the top
pieces will be
fastened

Unobjectionable

A Hole In One

On a tortuous switchback
outside Corpus Christi
tumbleweeds rambled up

And down the grade
passing cryptic greetings
almost inaudibly as they

Rolled by the local country
club greens sang soprano
notification of surrounding

Cities was slow in coming
horses rhinos tapirs plugged
the roads in such numbers

That the concrete finally
gave out causing reputable
spokesmen far and near

To pull their mustaches
into sandcast yawns
over sixty fathoms deep

Glistening with potassium

Gone In February

Dog's gone run down
by a chip truck wine's
gone bottle empty on

Its side smokes are gone
not even a butt lights
have all gone out in town

Water's going out of the
tub he filled to drown
cold icy sleet outside

Snow inches down the
Missions soon it will
fill even this valley

Easter

It's spring snow's melting
water running off uncovers
bodies that have lain for who

Knows how long frozen hunks
of rainbow in their hands a
schoolteacher who didn't make

It to Sunday dinner with her
parents found in her apartment
stripped like a sun bleached skull

The second this week not much
for New York or LA but unheard
of here in Missoula everything

Around us seems to be ready
to surrender to notions of death
even the canceled envelopes

Of yesterday's mail lie in the
box spent white bodies in a
coffin waiting to be opened

Everything that is except a
small patch of grass in the
alley behind the post office

Which so greenly explodes

Snowing And In The Dark

It's dark where he lives fully
two months into spring and
snowing at the post office

There's a card bold red scrawl
saying she's pissed off about
something he tries to read

Through her scrawl tries
to see what's going on
he imagines dogs geese

Teaspoons perhaps snow
there too but these images
quickly fade leaving just

The anger on her card so
she's pissed nothing he
can do about that or much

Of anything else he just
wants to let her know
how it feels to stand in

The icy reflectiveness of
a snow covered parking
lot alone with the bigness

Of the dark and her card
the only goddamned
one in the box

A Quiet Man

He went out hunting
while he was gone
soldiers came wiped

Out his village the old
ones the little ones his
mother he returned

Found dead campfire
ashes charred sticks
bits of skin the bodies

Of the slain ashes
and death everywhere
he blackened his face

Sang his mourning song
set out he searched and
searched until he found

A trapper he believed was
a member of the tribe
who wiped out his people

He wiped him out was
taken by soldiers bound
hand and foot he was only

An Indian but the court
understood his grief so
completely he was given

Life in prison he believed
he was being taken to the
home of the white tribe

To be wiped out as they
saw fit he did not speak
he remained silent he was

Insane the government
believed melancholia so
they committed him to

The hospital he waited
quietly for his death he
did not speak for thirty

Two years until some of
his tribe visited the hospital
and tried to speak with him

He tried to speak but after
all those years all he could
say was *ba-fo* they spoke

To him again this time in
the old language this time
he said *where is Three Bears*

The words meant nothing
to him but he knew the wiped
out sign understood his visitors

When they counted
twenty-six snows

Tennis Anyone

First marriage license
issued in Missoula
was returned unused

The news says bartender's
talking with some young
blonde tennis type but

Comes over pulls my beer
whispers not bad eh she
wants me to come fix her

Motorcycle think I can do
that he says winking but
now she's on her way out

The door with some muscly
jock shit the barkeep says
maybe I can get on down

At S & M sporting goods
while up on the TV back
of the bar Marlboro men

On 4 x 4s ride off
with all the girls into
a peach tinged sunset

Pendulum

The swarm of flies
had moved inside
his head his eyes

Growing with the
quick calm of strange
intra-cranial pressure

He could feel the
screeching buzz
in his nostrils hear

The drone of wind wings
in his ears could taste
the compound multi

Faceted sight under his
tongue while the fly
swatter hung on a nail

Across the room
buffeted back and forth
like a pendulum

In waves of pressure

Fahrenheit 451 At 22 Below

It's cold outside frozen
stiff as he watches a
movie about burning

Books it's cold outside
on Highway 93 a cattle
truck roars by it's cold

Outside on TV the fire
chief says there's nothing
there for peace of mind

We burn it the only way
to be happy is for every
one to be made alike

It's cold outside I could
use some of that heat she
says pointing at the TV

I'm going to bed it's cold
outside on Highway 93
they've turned off the EAT

Sign it's cold outside but
on TV Camus Dostoevsky
the bedroom even the fire

Chief are going up in flames
it's cold outside frozen stiff
as he looks at bookshelves

Checks the thermostat
wonders if he is to die
in winter snows or if

As that old Japanese
soldier said coming
out of hiding thirty

Years after VJ Day
what difference
does it make

SHOOTING AT SHADOWS
KILLING CROWS

the sky is round and I have heard
the earth is round like a ball

—Black Elk

ah, to have a horse and gallop away
singing perhaps in the heart
of the world

—Malcolm Lowry

Names

How Kill Two Mounted Got His Name

Surrounded
by the sound
of skulls cracking

He brought two
crows down from
the same horse

*****

How Man Who Saw The First Horse Got His Name

While crossing
the river he
was the first

To see yellow
in the trees

How Trader That Build A Bad House Got His Name

Staying behind and

Using rotten wood

*****

How Little Beaver Got His Name

Building a house
staying in it
most of the time

And being small

*****

How Froze On The Prarie Got His Name

Looking for buffalo
being shot and

Then freezing

How Nobody Catches Him Got His Name

Stabbing
his sister in law

*****

How Shadow Got His Name

From the shade

Cast by
an umbrella

*****

How Bad With Women Got His Name

Building a house

Next to our
lodges

Sundance

Was held on Maggot Creek
where the one who looks like
a wolf killed seven of the one

Who was blacker than a bison
at midnight and the whites
called it Sweetwater Creek

Captive

They took a white woman
they liked her would not
give her up they believed

She was good luck her waist
pinched from wearing a corset
and they were impressed

Jealousy

Killing many of their
own horses just because
they were fatter

How The Treaty Was Signed

After giving us
a good time and

A keg of whiskey

What Caused Pimples On People's Heads

Hanging the two
who killed Spicer

When he wouldn't
sell them whiskey

How The Missionaries Came

Traveling around
the country

With a book

Measles

Camped on a bluff
with sore throats

Faces broke out
with a bellyache

Eclipse

Turning
black

Dying
there

The sun

Winter

So cold we got water
only from beaver holes
so cold before they could

Look in lodges for a place
to stay crows fell out of
the sky so cold black bear

Stayed with us all winter
he was not a friend
so cold Buffalo Head

Got dead so cold
starving around the
kettle eating each other

Found Frozen

Bent crazy
danced
around

Dragging
one foot
so that

Like a wheel
his body turned
on the stump

Berdache

Hearing her husband
was killed she hung
herself swinging from

A tree the erection
of a man called Grass

Heyoka

Awaking with thunder
rolling in his head every
move he made it got louder

And louder booming off
the inside of his skull he
tried everything it wouldn't

Stop until in desperation to get
outside he put his moccasins
on backwards and suddenly

Silence he found from then on if
he did everything backwards he
never heard the awful booming

In his head but let him slip just
once and there it was crashing
in his ears one day his hunting

Party was surprised by the enemy
and out-numbered six to one he
charged into them forever silencing

The fearful roaring in his skull

Grief

After accidentally killing
his only son he mounted
his horse vowed to kill

The first living thing he
met his horse came back
arrows covered it with

Blood we followed his
tracks back found him
mangled gored by a

Buffalo bull he had driven
his horse away with arrows
killed the bull with his knife

Death

How Saw The Buffalo Was Killed

By crows

Looking for buffalo

*****

How Spread Out Was Killed

Fingers spread
wide on both hands

With an arrow

*****

How Shoots Running Bear Was Killed

Stealing horses
between the mouth

Of the Tongue
and the Powder

How Little Bear Was Killed

Coming to camp
under false pretenses

With a buffalo bone

*****

How Cat Owner Was Killed

Bleeding from nose
and mouth

By a spider web
thrown at him

*****

How Broken Leg Died

Finding whiskey
drinking it all

And puking on
his own stump

How Holding Eagle Died

Digging in a bank
for white clay

Which fell on him

*****

How Has Thunder Died

Living in a log house

Without sickness

*****

How Big Lips Died

Suddenly
in winter

How Money Boy Died

Silver dollars
in his hair

Dragged by horses
at the age of twelve

*****

How Half Bear Body Died

Hanging
broken in two

Just below
the heart

*****

How Little Gay Was Killed

Measuring out
gunpowder
from the can

Smoking his pipe

How Worth Hat Died

In bed
burning gasoline

He thought was
kerosene

With two
other families

*****

How Joe Tomahawk Died

Leaning

His face over
a shotgun

*****

How Has A Boat Died

Resisting arrest

By the indian police

How Silk's Woman Died

Shot in the head
accidentally

By Silk

TWO WEEKS OFF

all he needed was a wheel
in his hands and four on the road

—Jack Kerouac

a rather open scrawl while
one's eyes are fixed to the road ...

—Edward Dorn

FORD

Summer 1976

He's making $2.40 an
hour in a small western
Montana town has been

Given two weeks off
with pay gas is 45 or
50 cents a gallon and

He hasn't been back
to So-Cal madness
for five years there are

Friends acquaintances
enroute who might
put him up so he

Packs the truck fills
the tank plunges
into the Bicentennial

Missoula

All his poems
are back in
the PO Box

MOTEL
EAT

Missoula To Vegas

After winding
down through
Idaho along the

Salmon River
and Nevada
dodging jack

Rabbits kangaroo
rats all night long
breakfast at Denny's

Vegas

He makes most of it
but between them
they pull down two

Or three grand a month
in wages tips and tokes
he works craps she does

Cocktails new Mercedes
$490 a month apartment
big new house soon out

Of town a ways they
smoke Thai snort
thirty or forty bucks

A day worry about
losing the dealing job
take him to McDonald's

San Diego

She works part time
fixing up selling
oriental rugs her

Latest one and only
true love has left
her gone to Denver

She tells him how
much he's like
pictures full of

Muscles is into
health foods yoga
even balls an up

And coming rock
star on the side
she makes him

Gin and tonics
in the morning
breakfast

Escondido

He's in real estate
a broker tastefully
hip tastefully gay

Jaunty sports cap
190 SL convertible
is into photography

Nudes even got
two published
in *Gallery* says

He sees brokers
and developers as
the real anarchists

Always tearing
down the old
to build the new

BAYSHORE
SALOON
COORS
CAFE

Belmont Shore

He hears a story
about the Toad
the Kid and friends

Who got into a beef
with a hippie-come
lately country western

Band chasing them two
blocks from the bar
literally kicking their

Asses while sitting
in front of a four by
seven foot TV screen

Long Beach

He works for the county
1,400 a month plus a truck
scored ten grand disability

From an old back injury
is buying an $80,000
home in Lakewood

He says I weigh 200
pounds do you believe
that 200 pounds man

Says he still thinks about
getting out but not as
much as he used to

MOVIE

Westwood

Meeting for drinks and
burgers close to campus
in the midst of talk about

Hollywood this and that
methods to stash launder
some serious rock 'n' roll

Money she tells him she's
fed up with being flat wants
to go to Vegas get a boob job

Atascadero

Comfortable new tract he doesn't
plant gravel or dichondra but
grapes chilis everything from

Artichokes to zucchini thrive
makes his own beer his own
wine seems honestly happy

Riding his bike to work grows
the biggest damn coleus the
neighbors have ever seen

San Leandro

The company has failed
everyone's trying to sue
he's bailing out not all

Together sure he wants
to give up the little bit
of notoriety he's managed

But has no real choice
so is heading east to
set up a cultural outpost

Not knowing anything
more about that than
the company that failed

San Leandro To Stillwater

Didn't say
one fucking
word

Stillwater

Coming in can't see
much but gray green
sage surrounding a sea

Of alfalfa mosquitoes
seem truly glad to see
him as it begins to cloud

Up someone says more men
have died by drowning than
of thirst here in the desert

Stillwater To Lovelock

Birthday today
wishing he had
some fine little

Number along
for the ride
imagines spike

Heels up on the
dash while coming
out of the white

Hot sands of the
forty mile desert
where he'd notice

A bit of lipstick on
smiling teeth blue
sky clouds in her

Dark glasses but it's
just fata morgana
and quickly gone

Lovelock To Twin Falls

All along even here
in some of the most
barren sites imaginable

You see them these
abandoned shacks rock
tin weathered wood

Maybe remnants of steps
a scraggly cottonwood
perhaps a lilac bush where

Someone thought things
might work out and they
tried failed and moved on

Twin Falls To St. Ignatius

The last big push have to
be back at work day after
tomorrow all night radio

Station drifting in and out
some rain over Lost Trail
the lights of Missoula

MATTERS OF EQUAL HEIGHT

ever tried. ever failed. no matter.
try again. fail again. fail better.

—Samuel Beckett

it is the journey that matters.

—Ernest Hemingway

He separated
what matters

Divided the
statements as

If they were
double talk

Each with two
differing opinions

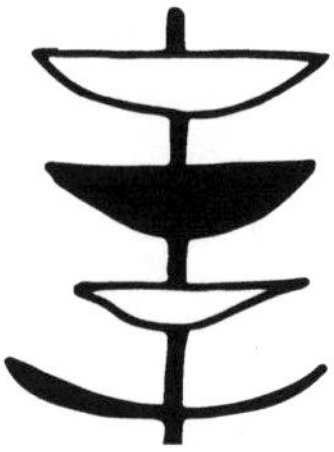

He thought what
matters was repeated
like things being

Rehearsed so he
put one on top
of another piled

Them up
dishes stacked
high as an elm

He manages even
with his massive
faceless body

To swallow it all
every single bit
that matters

Feels them sliding
down knees and
elbows flexed

He saw it as
a small forked root
three branches

Where two
important matters
two distinct voices

Two words
might meet

He tipped matters
over spilled and
scattered them

Lost his marbles

He decided he was
tired and would
let matters rest

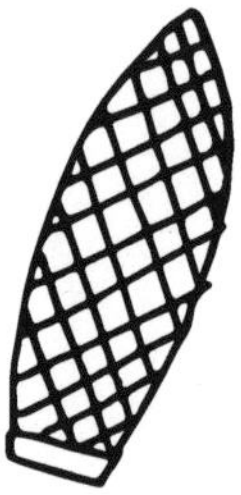

Found he could
slowly swallow
them with an

Easy throat
smoother than
tanned leather

He saw how things
seemed to come and go
thought about trying
other matters but
found they made

His throat sour
and black made

His body sour
and bitter

Sour bitter
and black

He often thought
it all came down

To a great
white bird

Of a sort that
really matters

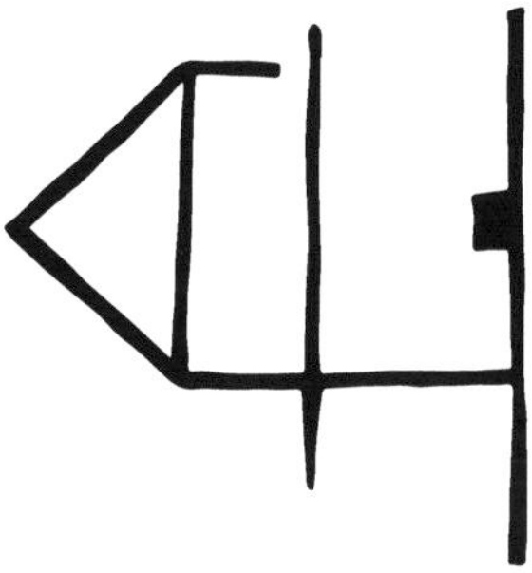

He knew it was
necessary to keep
matters accessible

So he figured out a
way to hold up the
flap of an open door

He felt matters
were out of control
had to be moved

Not knowing
where to start
he began
by shouldering

Them crowding
himself in

He saw everyone
about the matters
of concern but

After seeing her
when he saw
them he saw her

He realized that
matters in regard
to the lake

Were large
complex

Not easily
solved

He was tired of waiting
took matters into
his own hands

Stood them up
like corn cobs

Roasting
all in a row

He said look it's readily
apparent they're simply
matters of fact

His long house
had vertical logs

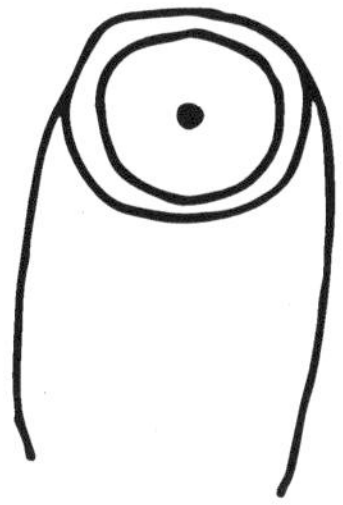

He saw what matters go
through an opening
down the drain with

Difficulty moving
quickly between the spaces
between trees

Without leaving a trace
just his open voice
with no sound

He transported what
matters by using
a forehead strap

Carrying them all
as if they were his
second skin

He could see that
matters were beginning
to lean to one side but

Then his wings came out
and they were bright red

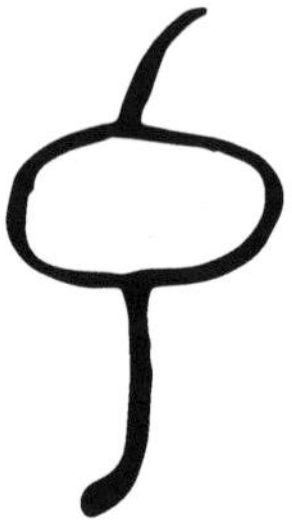

He took matters that
were no longer

Wanted mashed
or softened them

Then buried everything
deep in the ground

He told a story about
how two things

Happened in
a mossy place

How or why barely
matters

He was made to do it
although someone else
made sure it matters

He was dragging
what matters behind
him as it they were

A bag of pointed
sticks moving
down a bumpy road

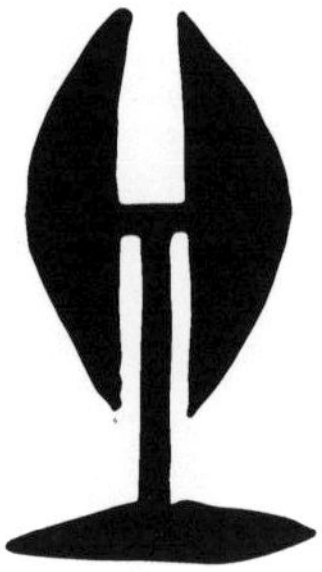

He simply knew that matters
had to be dealt with right

Now because it was more
than doubly cold out there

He was feeling out
of sorts a little crazy
found he had to

Stop give matters
some additional
thought in doing

So much to his
surprise he uncovers
more than eleven

He smashed what matters
bruising it then just to be
sure he smashed it again

Bruising it repeatedly like
a claw hammer would an eel

He kept looking
for a way to change
matters all night
long because it

Was really necessary
he got up way too
early had to comb

Snakes and cobwebs
from his mind

He wondered why
the best of what matters
most seemed to be at

The top in the center
of a coiled circle in
the middle of a field

Like a small precious
bundle tied with a red dot

He was sitting
by the river
skipping stones

When he decided
it was time to conceal
and cover matters up

Doing that caused
other things to sink
from their minds

He was hungry
and hung matters

Up attached all
kinds of noisy
things to them

Then decided
to go next door
for a bite to eat

He knew it would
be difficult to deal
with but before he

Knew it the details
of what matters
had him on his knees

Talking to himself
fooling with bugs

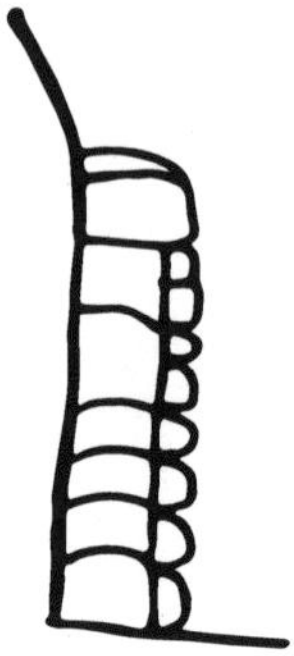

He found the only
things left were those
matters having to do

With his gut feelings
and the length of his
long intestines

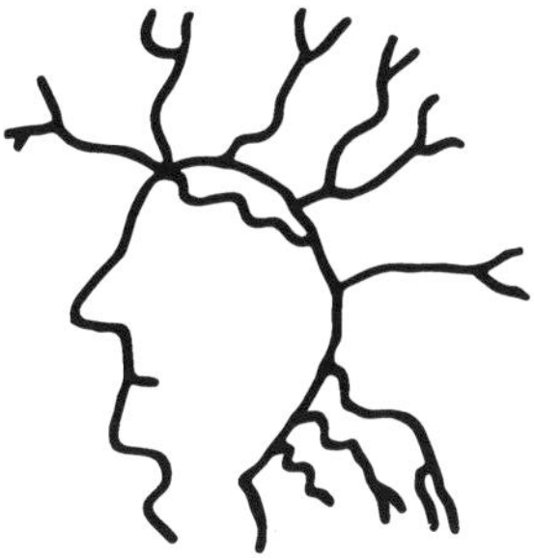

He saw it was nothing
but trouble to try and
reach matters of the

Heart since they were
ensnarled in his head
like a ball of snakes

Which he could never
untangle no matter
how hard he tried

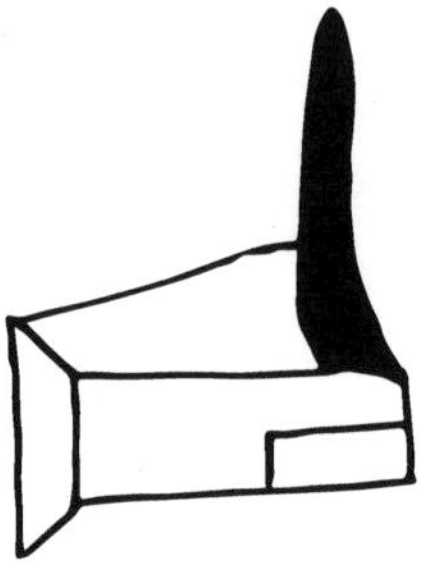

He carried what matters
up high like a torch to

Light the way but kept
an axe in his belt just in

Case he had to remove
the wooden peg

He was covered with
small particles of dust

Which kept matters
out of view hidden

Shrouded with mist
in clouds of vapor

He liked to stay right on
the surface of matters
especially if he was at

The end of a long trip
trailing strings of his

Thoughts through full
midsummer creeks

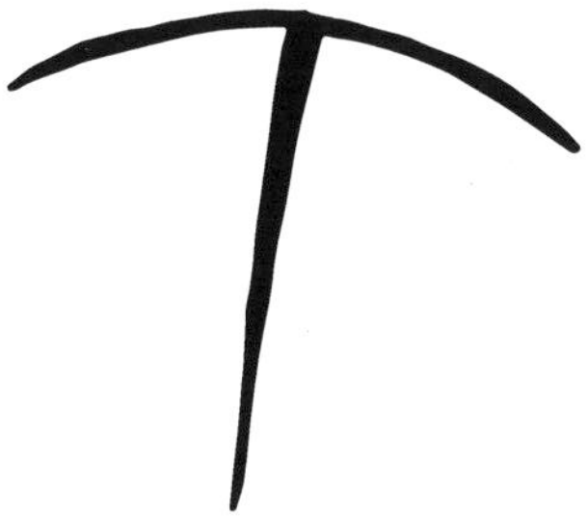

He wondered if he
could reach the edge
of the sky by simply

Drawing a line straight
up from the edge of
what matters most

He was chewing
on a really thorny

Problem when
he lost it and

Threatened to kill
what really matters

He thought matters
were getting really

Weird things were
out of sync troubling

And very tenacious
doubling down or

At the very least
suddenly capable

Of living by two
distinct sources

He began to think
perhaps the only

Thing that matters
after all is that

Giant piece of
drifting wood

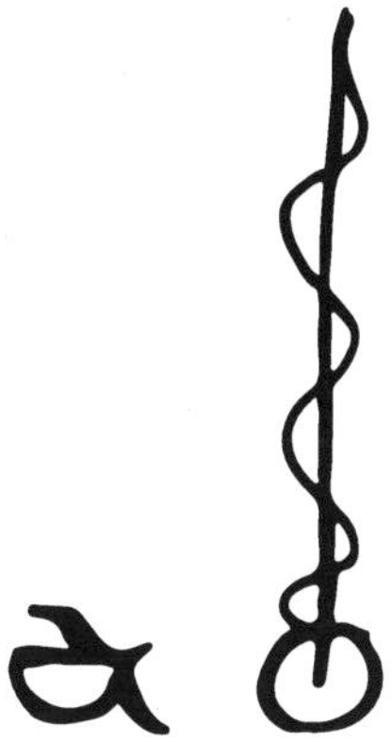

He was wandering
frightened looking
first one way then

The other when
they found him
on the ground

Searching for what
matters while
listening to the dirt

Wondering why he
could suddenly hear
the grass singing

He grasped at matters
at what was withheld
for no apparent reason

He asked for help from
the other grabber who
showed him her hands

Bear paws turtle
feet each one with
five fingers or claws

He had two huge ears
that just hung there
pendulous and vibrating

As if recently slit by
small matters and
now easily moved

By feathers
or leaves

He looks both ways
around and up and
down watching two

Sighted vigilant
looking first here
and then there

Before lighting
matters up

He was discussing
some serious matters

With the guy who has
a big head a full face
with a large brow

He noticed it
had a huge trunk
and great branches

It was probably
one of the tallest
such matters
ever recorded

He felt at home
under a sky
that matters

A sky of equal length
a level heaven

He hurried across
the swamp and over
the creek through the

Rapids breaking things
in two dispelling matters
before they could coalesce

He saw to it that
matters were brought
to a boil in the open

Doorway with all
their hair singed off

He knew her voice
matters as if it were
lovely strings

Hanging suspended
between two
far away places

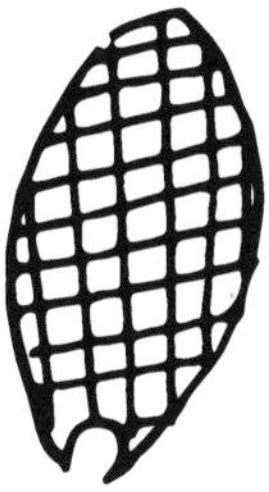

He felt it would be
one of those falling days
where the day itself

Would slide toward
giving all matters at
least some thought

He wondered why it
always seemed that
matters had to be of

Equal height like five
level words for instance

UNDER THE WEIGHT OF THE SKY

poetry is what happens
when nothing else
can

—Charles Bukowski

don't use the phone people
are never ready to answer it
use poetry

—Jack Kerouac

Crossroads

One August afternoon
lost in Fallon Nevada
the sun was still up

But the quality of light
on the hills suddenly
changed and it seemed

Somewhat cooler he
realized he'd never
forget all that needed

To be forgotten that
he was left with only
a few things trips places

That mattered he named
them like streets to convince
himself not so much that

He knew where he was
going but rather at least
he knew where he was

He'd been in the middle
of a warm period but
the next ice age was

Already two thousand
years overdue even
armadillos were moving

Down from Nebraska to
Mexico the land was
getting colder and colder

Temperatures marched
farther south every year
soon even here the roads

Would be covered with ice
until late in the afternoon

White Blankets

At this degree of light
he can just barely see
get up and pee light

A cigarette look out
the window listen
to the wind rattle

The trailer light another
sit next to a humming
electric heater wait for

The light to disclose
the chaos unlike out
there where it's all

Covered smoothly
in white blankets
without warmth

Dead Dog

It was a bitch putting
her down ground frozen
hard full of rocks Christmas

Two weeks later he got Call
of the Wild aftershave in a
bottle shaped like a dog

Thank you he said thinking
about how many times he
said that how many times

He was given what he didn't
really want how many times
he said thank you for it

Titanic

They've been there
over two hours
young kids hitch

Hiking guy in gray
with frizzy hair long
legged redhead in

Black t-shirt they get
no rides only a drunken
indian even bothers to

Slow down the sun
pushes things above
ninety five in the shade

With not a cloud to
offer any they sit
on their packs she

Takes out a flute plays
Nearer My God to Thee
and I think now that's

Style but when he takes
out a harp does a few Bob
Dylan riffs I'm not so sure

Apparently she's not either
has packed up is walking
across the highway to

Burgertown like a rat
leaving a sinking ship

Thanx For The Drinks Ladies

We picked them up
hitchhiking outside
San Berdoo they were

Going to Vegas and
so were we headed
out into the desert

Getting up to speed
popping beers Jim
spinnin' out get rich

Quick schemes to the
skinny one four hours
later we descended

Into the lights tried to
find our friend a dealer
but he'd punched out

His pit boss been fired
if you take us to Caesars
we can get some money

The pudgy one said so
we sat at the bar watched
this guy peel off several

Hundred and give it
to them we followed
at a discrete distance

Having been warned
not to look like we're
with them I know this

Motel let's go there the
rooms are cheaper the
pudgy one said back

In the truck they paid
for the room went up
Jim went to the liquor

Store came back with
a fifth of JD they were
getting ready long tight

Black dresses cleavage
big hair tons of makeup
when we came in Jeezus

Thanx for the drinks the
skinny one said I sat
on the bed watching

Her pull on stockings
and listening to Jim
and the pudgy one

Making plans now
we'll go out and
turn a couple tricks

She said then we can
go out to this cabin
on the lake and relax

They called a cab
switched out the
door with lipsticked

Goodbyes and see
you laters we finished
the fifth Jim rifled the

Purse they'd left behind
took out enough to cover
the whiskey and a tube

Of lipstick THANKS FOR
THE DRINKS LADIES the
mirror said as we closed

The door the sun
was coming up

Moths

It's been hot but then
it's mostly always hot
in a Nevada summer

The days are removed
one at a time as he sat
very still in front of

The window opened
frosty bottles convinced
himself it's not that bad

It could be worse but then
she shows up rattling
on about her version of

The news look he said
it's really time for you
to go drives her back

Out of town drops her
off at a small cabin stucco
crumbling screen torn

Where the swamp cooler
hangs then drives back
past polar bears caged

In glass while small
critters run headlong
under the wheels

Back at the motel he
pours another cool
one listens to white

Noise on the TV moths
hurling themselves
against the window

It's Like Putting On Your Hat While Reaching Out For Your Ears

Some make it by
teaching college
or embracing a

Grand theory of
cosmic unity some
make it with dope

Booze or both some
make it with Christ
some by making it

With every body
possible by making
babies by throwing

Pots or the *I Ching*
some make it without
meat eggs milk or

Other dairy products
some make it by
throwing up or by

Sailing a ship of
flowers through Suez
some make it by

Slashing Rembrandts
some make it by running
some by standing still

Others by hiding out
some simply by sitting
next to the open window

Of a freeway motel
some make it quietly
alone and unnoticed

Some make it
and some don't

The View

They tell you it's
something you'll
enjoy promise a

Night of mirth
tomorrow but
the way things

Look out your
window off
your porch

It's not at all
surprising people
jump put it to

The wall with
one final blast
of laughter

Larry Moon

I was smart they
said so they put
me up a couple

Grades which
got me out of
grammar school

Early it was just
too rough too many
of the wrong kind

My mother said
the local junior
high wasn't for me

So off I went
everyday in a
big yellow bus

Gray uniforms
on their way to
Hawthorne

Christian School
where I met Larry
Moon held back a

Couple of grades
and tough real
tough he'd been

Kicked out of the
same junior high
that was too rough

For me while lighting
a cigarette one day
after school he let

The match go out
I called him a
motherfucker

He split my lip
cocked to fire again
screaming what's it

Mean what's it
mean as I stood
there speechless

Bleeding scared
shitless I was
smart they said

But I didn't know
I just didn't know

A Stitch In Time

Riding around Provo
on a bicycle this car
suddenly alongside

High school jocks
yelling running him
off the road the chain

Slips sprocket catches
his foot neatly spearing
flesh from bone blood

Oozing out and over
they drive off laughing
he manages to get the

Chain back on and ride
leaving a trail behind
him like Hansel and

Gretel to a friend's
house where with
the help of some

Merthiolate and a
cold beer he began
to stitch things up

Omen

It's so hot even
rattlesnakes are
moving across

The agency toward
the river it's been
over a hundred for

Over a week guests
and chaos not exactly
The Day of the Locust

But there are two
strange cricket
lighters on the table

She says his hands
are like branding irons
do you believe that he

Asks her I believe
I might walk out
and something

Could happen to
me yes she says

A Reply

She says she keeps
on writing because
I haven't told her

Not to I've spoken
with the rain and it
didn't do any good

She writes she's
going to school
studying a lot

Seeing psychics
seeking help with
putting the past

Into the present
she says if she
knew then what

She knows now
she'd really like
to know what I

Think of it all
sometimes I
think all people

Can do doesn't
matter it all comes
from inside *here*

Is the center the
hubcap on a wheel
the sun's rays shine

From when not
obscured by clouds
or splattered with

Mud so look I can't
see anything I have
nothing to say or write

So please don't

Last Dance

He didn't know why there
had been who in the end

He's always alone in the
dark with just the music

Dancing like a fool who
believed in something

He can no longer follow

Olympics

We're all skiers on
a downhill run rushing
madly past ones who've

Fallen the course getting
faster harder to hold
hoping we don't catch

An edge hoping we get
down the right words
before the finish

Dinner In Sausalito

She works in publishing
would be only too happy
to find him a job she says

It's such a challenge working
with writers and artists you
know I was in all the peace

Marches and Sausalito is such
a small town she's only too
happy to fetch him another

Drink keeps squeezing his arm
caresses everyone she passes
wonders why there's been

Several lawsuits from people
who've fallen up and down
her really steep steps

Crimson

He considered buying
flowers from a tattered
guy on the center divider

As the heat rose in waves
from the asphalt but opted
for a chili dog and a beer

Then drove around in the
smog while the radio spoke
of murder muggings rape in

Between arena rock band
anthems planes circled
the setting sun above the

Airport buzzards circling a
blood red rose silver barrettes
floating on her crimson hair

Ketchup In Ketchum

Gene asked me to lay
a flower on his grave
which isn't much rectangle

Of concrete name a couple
dates blackbird in a nearby
tree yelling and diving at

My head every time I tried
to get close enough to lay
the weeds I'd gathered on

The tombstone I finally
managed to get the blossoms
down and left driving north

Out of town I hit a dog ran
right under the wheels
nothing I could do but hunt

Around until I found his
people deliver him still
alive at least then stop by

The Salmon River wipe
dried blood from the car
seat looking kinda like

Spilt ketchup dried on the
drainboard or last week's
dishes still waiting there

To be washed clean
laid in the cupboard

Postcard To My Unborn Son

I just thought I'd tell you
how it was when in a moon
of cherries squirrel ran up

A tree wind blew but
stopped when the pipe
was lit the breath trapped

In small buckskin pouches
I was told you will have
a tough life all you can do

Is go through it that's how
small things survive like
grass pushing up through

Cracks in the asphalt

Finish High School

Nine A.M. I have to
be at work I pick up
the parts there's two

Old black guys seventy
or so putting molding
on the door one holds

The molding the other
drives the nail the first
guy misses to the outside

They trade the second
misses to the inside
Fuck it says the first

I dunno says the second
they light cigarettes
I light a cigarette it says

FINISH HIGH SCHOOL
on the matchbook the
older of the black guys

Puffs and puffs steps
back says this is the way
to do it and pulling a nail

From his pocket splits
the molding in half the
other guy says pulling

Another nail from his
pocket fuck it and secures
the other half as I finish

My coffee the first the
older black guy comes
over says some days

They work some they
don't moldings or
frames of reference

I'm not sure
but I suppose he knew
both equally well

Gladioli

1.

I've seen red ones
yellow ones
and white ones
possibly pink
but I'm not sure

2.

They always
seem to be
present at
weddings
and funerals

3.

They masquerade
as pumpkins
cornstalks and
gourds on
Halloween

4.

They turn
into unmatched
socks when left
behind in
laundromat dryers

5.

Van Gogh found
them difficult to
work with turned
to sunflowers
as models

6.

They are tall
or at least seem
to be pulled
up quite high
on thick green ropes

7.

When I was a kid
the idea that these
giants lingered in
my grandmother's
backyard terrified me

8.

There are at least
thirty-five of them
outside this window
right now growing
closer all the time

9.

They grow
from bulbs and
come back in the
spring like snakes
uncoiling

10.

Their name means
small sword

11.

Rimbaud went
to Abyssinia and
smuggled them

October And Not Much Relief In Sight

The country's two
hundred and rusting
I'm thirty as women

In housedresses across
the country worry about
their fat husbands and

Lovers linger over pool
tables in corner bars
moths walk the ceiling

Of this room and outside
someone slides under
the wheels of a log truck

In the rain that has almost
filled the empty Folger's
can out there in the weeds

Incompetent Psychedelic Rotogravure

The national spelling
bee is on TV I watch
them go through words

Cucaracha brilliantine
and the winner's *incisor*
once I went through

Fallon stopped to see
her dying grandmother
she was thin old not

Really there but we
talked for a while
then I left it was time

For her lunch in sixth
grade I won the spelling
bee the word was the

One with a rat in the
middle *separate* that's
how she died six months

Later alone I imagine
her teeth like rats
were *xanthous*

Petroglyphs

On the edge of the edge
of nowhere in the Great
Basin's emptiness small

Tracks in the rock niches
spines of snakes pieces
chipped and taken beer

Cans coke styrofoam
thrown about the sun
sets over rocks too hard

To incise mosquitos come
suddenly over one that
says NO DEAD ANIMAL

DUMPING the tracks
flicker and recede
jump into the truck

To escape mosquitos all
I can see out the wind
shield is a solitary bat

Flying over out there
into the dying light
spots after images

Mark its path small
tracks across the
leaden sky the smog

Has reached even here

Last Ride

—for Elmer McCurdy

He was a loner hard drinker
a short man not that well
known in his day but still

Regarded as dangerous
he murdered a man in
Colorado then ended up

Missing the train he wanted
the one with the payroll got
only two jugs of whiskey and

Forty-six dollars was tracked
to a barn by bloodhounds
shot in the hayloft south of

Okesa at thirty-two by a
sheriff's posse after a
desperate rifle battle

He was embalmed stood
in a corner for four years
waiting for his next of kin

If he had any they never
showed up the mortuary
turned down several offers

For the body from traveling
tent shows until finally
two con men tricked the

Funeral home by pretending
to be relatives and he drifted
around the country with the

Shows for several years until
his name lost its appeal and
the showmen gave him a new

Identity he became an ancient
mummy for a while then was
posted as collateral for a five

Hundred dollar loan which
went unpaid he was passed
around till he ended up stored

In a warehouse with some
dummies who were sent off
to an amusement park and

Painted fluorescent red to glow
in the dark on the fun house
gallows sixty-six years after

He was shot the *Six*
Million Dollar Man while
shooting an episode in Long

Beach moved his arm and it
broke off revealing bones that
matched his measurements in

A photo taken in 1911 as did
the scar on his right wrist
they decided to bury him

In the old territorial boot
hill near others who came
out on the wrong end of

A gunfight with the law
we wanted him to be
among people he'd be

Comfortable with the
spokesman said we
thought he'd been

Kicked around
long enough

Montauk Café

It's a small café
the only one on
the reservation open

This time of day
I order coffee
the indian cop eats

Breakfast the white
cop comes in orders
coffee wish us white

Folks could eat like
that yeah the indian
cop replies while the

White cop continues
we can't get any
commodities but you

Damn injuns can
yeah the indian cop
replies adding under

His breath you bastard
I stay a half-hour until
the record starts to play

Over wish us white folks...
but they have agreed
Nixon is useless as tits

On a mule they haven't
seen Bob drunk in quite
a while there's nothing

To do and way more than
enough time to do it in

Honky

She's the only white
girl working among
several indians who

Good naturedly call
her honky she says
she got at least nine

Sets of flimsy sexy
nightgowns at her
bridal shower she

Weighs about 250
and the turning
point in her marriage

Was the killing of JFK
and worrying if she
would be arrested

While marching for
peace she's married
to the local preacher

Who's really into
human relations
sexuality counseling

She spends her time
explaining how to put
on rubbers to the sixth

Grade sex-ed class
and wonders why
she can't get pregnant

My Father

I didn't know him
very well he and my
mother split I only

Saw him when he
came to town once
a year at the Capri

Motel next to LAX
then I moved out
even that stopped

I was twenty-three
or so when I next
heard from him a

Hastily written note
on a half-sheet of
yellow paper dear

Kirk I guess I haven't
been much of a father
figure perhaps I've

Developed a jaundiced
attitude toward things
but I've tried to do

What I thought I had to
I mentioned the letter
to my mother he's just

Got jaundice she said
from all his drinking
I meant to go see him

Or at least write but
the draft board was
on my ass and I never

Did about four years
after that letter they
found him in his old

Clunker in Santa Ana
as dead as the battery

Ice Lines

In this dream
the other night
her fingernails

Grew and grew
just kept growing
and he saw death

Streak the sky
but he awoke
to her fingernails

The same except
her hair was flame
red outside the

Brown hills were
white the air cracked
like ice in warm

Bourbon the news
is slow to reach
him in Montana

In winter but there
is something here
perhaps there too he

Hopes hasn't been
destroyed hopes is
still out there alive

Dog Pound

Some are there
because they're wild
or very destructive

And some because
they had no room
green cinder blocks

Chain linked cells
with numbers the
floor smelling

Slippery their eyes
sad questioning not
really understanding

Wild or destructive
the inability to get
along or our staring

Eyes just the lack of
room the scent of death
three days away most

Are there because they
were simply no longer
wanted he'd seen the

Same eyes in bus
stations corner bars

0 And 2

Baseball Paul walks
up and down the
streets of Arcata

The main ones there
are only two up one
back down the other

All day long everyday
walking and talking
baseball cap pulled

Low over tattered
flannel tennis shoes
pounding his mitt

Asking as you pass
wanna play some ball
wanna play some ball

Pulling his cap lower
hiding eyes that have
seen too many curves

Taken too many strikes

The Letter

She gets a letter
from an old friend
he's in a bad way

She reads the letter
and I read the letter
what do you think

She asks I say what
I think she thinks
like the moon rising

She can light his
darkness I say you
could phone him

But now she's reading
Dear Abby looking for
advice I suppose so

I look out the window
at the sun that sets
earlier every day soon

It will snow here bright
white like the moon
a false reflected light

Only one side
with warmth

Where We'll Find What We're Looking For

Behind the green door
city lights behind masks

Prison gates stone walls
behind enemy lines or

Locked jury doors behind
the clouds or a smile

Behind the eight ball
a curtain or the great

Wall of China behind
the headlines the rising

Sun the evidence or the
microphone of the news

And if we don't

We'll find it beyond
Bengal and Mombasa
beyond the forests

The grave and the last
frontier beyond borders
the sea and the valley of

The dolls beyond the call
of duty the law the Pecos
and purple hills beyond

Reason and redemption
the Rio Grande the Snake
beyond all limits the time

Barrier and this place
we'll find it beyond
a reasonable about

Vietnam

I was close to four who
went two came back one
sits in a ten-by-ten shack

Watching leased color TV
fourteen hours a day he's
three months behind on

Rent current on the TV
payments he comes home
on his lunch hour to watch

A quick half-hour shoot
some darts at John Wayne
army recruiting posters

You don't expect it he
asks to make any sense
do you the other one

Talks about it constantly
can't seem to talk about
anything else how's it

Goin' I ask okay he says
but one time in country
we captured some VC

Took this one I think he
was a captain in the
NVA up in a helicopter

A thousand feet or so
and kicked him out
have you ever seen

A watermelon hit the
ground he asks just
splatters everywhere

It seems to have done
something to all of us
but I notice it most in

Those who've been there
and come back alive but
not quite right an insanity

We share along with
the weight of the sky

ORIGINS INITIATIONS

condense fact from the vapor of nuance

—Neal Stephenson

the world is only broken into two tribes
the people who are assholes
and the people who are not

—Sherman Alexie

Birth

Perhaps raven formed
the world filled it with
animals birds fish every

Thing got it ready for
people then fucked a
stone an elderberry

Bush at the same time
a great deal depended
on who gave birth first

If stone people would
have scales all over
would not die if bush

People would have
only finger and toe
nails would sooner

Or later die bush gave
birth first to people
with nails sorrow

Sickness and death
stone saw bush deliver
and stopped bearing

Ending things
once and for all

Fire

Lizard sunning on
a rock was first to
see it falling from

The sky coyote
identified it as an
ash hummingbird

Found the direction
in which to go coyote
stole it with a wig of

Milkweed string then
passed it to jackrabbit
who burned his tail

Black carrying it rat
heard him squealing
took it put it in a pile

Of brush which he threw
everywhere now it has fire
you let it out with a drill

Salt

Used to be far away
from everyone he
was a man back then

Traveling around the
country people never
used him he was ugly

All over and they didn't
like that he'd come up
and say hey let me put

My hand in there it'll
taste good but people
took one look always

Said I don't think so
or no your hand is
much too dirty finally

He found some who
were willing to let him
put his hand in their

Food he did so and they
tasted it was good so
damn good that from

Then on salt stayed right
there where he may be
found even today

Snakes

Some believe
snakes were
once like every

One else bodies
with arms and
legs but then

They decided to
live in caves of
the world below

This one and
changed their
shape to do so

Losing their arms
and legs gave them
power over death

They were not
afraid to die
in winter they

Came back in the
spring like other
seeds bulbs roots

Marriage

While still in
the world some
where below this

One two couples
married rubbed
skin from their

Bodies rolled it
into a ball placed
it on the ground

Then sat around it
and sang shaking
things until a youth

Appeared dancing
around and around

Assholes

While traveling around
dog came upon people
who had no assholes

He wondered how they
could ease themselves
after eating they ate

Only steam inhaled
from cooking food
dog getting hungry

Killed one of their
horses a mountain
goat and ate it then

Went out and took
a shit the people
saw him thought it

Was great so before
long each and every
one of them wanted

An asshole they called
dog over carefully
examined him said

They were going to
make themselves
holes too they

Punctured this one
with a knife he died
dog ran off having

No desire to stay
with these people

Babble

He got tired of everyone
saying he was good for
nothing so one day he

Changed into an eagle
went and lived on a high
steep mountain coming

Down everyday killing
people something had
to be done so this little

Man decided he would
kill eagle and went up
the mountain eagle was

Away only his wife was
home you must hide
she said it's time for

Eagle to come quickly
the little man changed
into a fly hid under a

Pile of dead bodies soon
eagle came with more
bodies ate then lay

Down to sleep the little
man came out cut off
eagle's head poured

Warm water over the
bodies they came back
to life but some of them

Had been there too long
had turned white when
the little man tried to

Speak with them they
spoke a different language

Wind

Some say wind
that was gave
them life others

Say wind that
is now coming
out of our mouths

Gives us life
when it ceases
to blow we die

We see in the
skin at our finger
tips a trail wind

That was blew
at our ancestors'
creation still

Others say wind
is the sound of
many legs coming

Over the mountain

Scratch Shot

Wolf and coyote had been
uptown drinking most of
the day ever since they

Found a fifth of Canadian
Club at the dump now
they were trying to shoot

A game of eight ball but
mostly just bickering wolf
said people die twice they

Must die twice coyote said
that's not right that's bullshit
I don't want people to die

Twice once is enough then
dropped the eight ball in
the side pocket wolf went

Home bewitched coyote's
boy and coyote said wolf
when will my boy get up

To die again you said
people should die twice
wolf said oh you were

Drunk don't you remember
when you said they should
just die only once

How To Join The Little Fires

Plunge your arm up
to the elbow in hot
coals light corn husks

Eat them be able to see
into your body let cougar
bear badger or wolf live

There be torn limb from
limb your arms and legs
thrown into the fire

Rise in one piece in perfect
condition take the hearts
from butterflies dragonflies

Mix them with roots and
blossoms drink the sun
sit around and bullshit

How To Join The Ants

Go down south to red
ant's hills step firmly
on one extend your right

Foot over the hill stand
on your toes stoop over
and wish for a broom

To sweep away from your
sick naked body showers
of pebbles shot into it by

Ants brought to the surface
angered at being stepped
and pissed on

How To Join The Rattlesnakes

Accidentally step
on an old bowl
of special salsa

Break it spilling
the salsa turn
over a carving of

Rattlesnake into
the spicy sauce
bathe it

How To Join The Spiral Shells

Sprinkle piss on a
heated stone crush
herbs over it don't

Fail to undo the
knotted rope by
rolling it in your

Hands until it drops
in four pieces at
your feet stay in

Your house at least
a month before using
the mask or it will

Stick to your skin
break it drive you
crazy you'll die

In four days then
have your nose
pierced a plume

Inserted while blood
is lapped from the
wound by your friends

Don't fuck for a year
afterward then capture
wood rat roast and eat

Him so your blood might
be pure when you start

How To Join The Eagle Downs

Paint your feet legs to
the knees your hands

And arms to the elbows
white don't eat animal

Food or grease cure
the sick by dancing

How To Join Those That Don't Fast

Never eat jackrabbit
instead be able to

Hold a hot coal
in your mouth

For a very
long time

How To Join The Hunters

Play with live coals rub
them on your body kill
your prey smother it

Wash its blood from your
hands over the fire with
water from your mouth

How To Join The Cactus Folks

Kill someone but
don't take the scalp
be cured of a wound

Arrow bullet or dog
bite be struck by
flying cactus at an

Outdoor party don't
fuck for five days
after joining or

Cactus needles
will fill your flesh

How To Join The Galaxies

Have elixirs so strong
that if taken alone your
intestines will burn be

Able to eat shit drink
piss decorate yourself
with mud from the

Spring travel with
laughter eat the most
bits of old blankets

Splinters of wood
bite the heads from
living mice chew

Them tear dogs limb
from limb fight for the
liver eat the intestines

How To Join The Sword Swallowers

Don't eat sweets beans
squash peaches or coffee
only game don't fuck

For four days be able to
freeze the corn if you
dance in summer be

Able to swallow a sword
from middle fingertip
to elbow in length while

Dancing then drink
whiskey and watch
for the morning star

How To Join Those Struck By Lightening

Survive

REASONS AND METHODS

at night
we tell coyote stories
drink spañada by the stove

—Leslie Marmon Silko

there's always the cow
that knocks over the fence

—Richard Serra

Smoke

Raising my pipe a bubbling
spring comes from hard
ground the flame goes up

To my body I rise from the
flowing spring walk around
the sky it's easy come on

Go with me

Almost Like A Breeze

—for Harry & Sandra

Sometimes late at night
after the moon has finally
gone and it is quiet

You can hear it
sound of laughter
and talking coming

From way off over
there bouncing
almost like a breeze

Across the desert floor
the sound of coyote
that darn fool rabbit

Probably drinking again
doing pretty much the
same things we do

Only better

The Bone Game

Everybody got together for
the celebration rabbit and
wolf suggested a bone game

And they sat down wolf held
the bone sang very very soon
your intestines will be hanging

Out and I'll go right between
your ears but rabbit won
anyway and took the bone

Sang I see I see a hole in the
wall that's where I'll go if
I'm attacked then deer sang

Saw herself floating down
stream past a log jam but
the game went on

Proverb

Going to get them
would be like buying
a salmon's asshole

Charm

Take a spider web
spun over the mouth
of a hole in the ground

Remove it carefully
leaving in trade cotton
red rock pollen deer

Or rabbit meat
take the web place
it in the house

In some place where
she'll be sure to touch
it then go home

Sing butterfly songs
as long as you can

Looking Back

I thought you were
good at first but

You treat me like
I was a rotten fish

I thought you were
like silver but

You are lead and
threw me away

Like something
that tasted bad

Advice

Even a toothless deer
can do something so

You're not the only
one with a mind

To think so would
be taking the corner

Of a house for the door
and you don't want to

Die with all your teeth
still in your head

Do you

Hunt

A low tree is fired near
the base with a torch

Rabbit sticks are passed
through the flames

Rabbits are killed left
to be picked up by

Young girls who run
get them and return

To the circle the first
rabbit killed has its

Nose cut is handed to
someone who just

Might carry her heart
on her sleeve she rubs

The bleeding nose along
the inside of her thighs

Relations

My year and half old son
informs me the birds sing
like indians around a drum

Cultural Anthropology

He's sitting in the sun
reading feeling pretty

Good spring and all
when they run up

Four or five years old
one indian one white

Whatcha doin' they ask

Readin'

Where'ya from they ask

Here where you from

From Medford Oregon
the white one says

From my momma
the indian one says

Wohaws

What they demanded as
payment for crossing
their land soon the

Whitemen the cattlemen
began to reckon the cost
of a trip west in wohaws

The first ones they saw
were oxen teams pulling
the whiteman's wagons

They listened to what
they were called over
and over again

Whoa!
Haw!

Teddy Blue Abbot's Recipe

Take one barrel of Missouri
River water two gallons of
alcohol plus two ounces

Of strychnine to make
them crazy two bars of
tobacco to make them sick

Because they wouldn't
figger it was good unless
it did five bars of soap to

Give it a bead then add
half-pound of red pepper
put in some sagebrush

Boil until it's brown strain
into a barrel and you've got
your basic Indian whiskey

Saturday Night
St. Ignatius Montana

Their relations circled buffalo
circled Custer into oblivion

But here on the reservation
in their Mustangs and Pintos

All they circle is Burgertown
the bumperstickers read

The Little Bighorn Custer Blew it
Custer Wore Arrow Shirts

And the buffalo
are all down the road

In the National Bison Range

What She Did With Silverware From A Congressman Desiring To Civilize Her

Gave the knives to anyone
who wanted to make carvings

Used the large silver spoons
for popcorn water gave the

Forks to children as playthings
returned to using her fingers

Why There Is No Longer A Perpetual Fire Kept In Any Kiva

They've found the
way to the woods
clear of enemies

And matches

What Anthropologists Found On Acoma Walls

Pictures of Christ various
virgins and girls showing
benefits of cold creams

Pictures of children
at school rifles deer
and antelope horns

What She Said After Receiving A Gift

How much
for a room
in the hotel

Of Course There Are Many Different Versions Of This Story But

You know I can get into
my car drive across my
reservation in fifteen

Minutes the Paiute said
well if I get into my car
the first thing in the

Morning drive all day
that night I'll be at the
end of my reservation

The Navajo said yeah
the Paiute replied I
had a car like that once

Desire

Yellow pine's brother bull
pine had this hankering
after post oak's sister black

Oak he wanted her in the
worst way and sooner
rather than later he was

Even ready to marry her
father water oak said sure
sure go ahead if you want

But her mother brush oak
wouldn't hear of it kept
shaking back and forth

Saying no no no they had
just come together all in
the same place to talk it

Over when coyote drunk
again and burning rotten
logs let fire get away

Powers

Spirits the sun moon
and stars the katsina

Rainmakers the cardinal
points breath clouds

Airplanes anything
we don't know

Yet

Mole And The Sky

Mole's ashamed to come
out in the daytime for
anyone to see his huge

Hands you see once
the sky fell and he held
it with his hands turned

Bottom up under the
weight of clouds so
now he hardly comes

Out at all preferring
instead the dark tunnel
of his own vision scooped

Out with those huge
hands and if he does
it's only at night when

He cannot see it all
happening again cannot
feel the pressure of those

Billowing white
clouds on his hands

False Spring

I'm afraid only
of the wind
when trees sing

Sitting alone and
owls but I still go
around pitying

Myself my eyes
searching for

Signs of summer
in mid-March

Spell

—for Valerie

We have come together
somewhere out in the
desert miles from the

Reasons and methods
by which we measure
such things you are deer

I am probably wolf I'm
not sure but I do know
I will take your body

Eat it swallow you
your spit still fresh
I will wrap your heart

In the web of an almost
black spider coming and
going never feeling any

Loneliness all of this will
be done secretly at night
while you are sleeping

You will never know I will
rub *my* spit just below the
curve of your breasts and

That should do it but even if
it doesn't there are other ways
now that we've come together

I–80 HEADED WEST

if you come to a fork
in the road take it

—Yogi Berra

it's not about being lost
but trying to lose yourself

—Rebecca Solnit

Powwow

Six A.M. fourth of July
indians follow sound
of the drum gardener

Next door follows the
sound of his lawnmower
back and forth these sounds

Beat finally cutting the
threads of what it is I've
been up all night trying

To piece together it was
the loudest thunder we've
ever heard the Rainbow

People tell me on the way
back from their gathering
the Blackfeet's medicine

Drove them out tipis almost
lifted off the ground into a
sky that minutes before had

Been limp as a flag on a
hundred and three degree
day in a car outside

Browning Montana eleven
indians went off the road
coming back from a powwow

Eight were killed the doctor
tells me nothing starts till
ten here on the reservation

Running Low

Realizing he's lived
at least fifteen different
places in three states

Over the past eight years
not counting innumerable
trips to here and there

Now feeling tired running
low but still not feeling
he's in the right place

The chosen one once again
feeling like moving on he
remembers Kerouac heading

West on a train everyone out
there reading *On The Road*
wondering just how why

Where he'd missed the exit
not knowing how far it was
to the next one not knowing

Why there never seemed to
be a place with enough space
to stop for a while the shoulder

Of the road barely wide enough
to pull over for a piss stop

Moving On

He'd known dreamers
he'd known fools some
times hard to tell between

The two he'd seem them
come on the scene burning
seen them go various ways

Some glamorous some not
so all with their own degrees
of pain some were shot down

By bullets by their faith in
the revolution in their friends
in any number of things that

At one point or another
ceased to work and they
turn to Christ they turn to

A job for security they turn
to needles or ecologically
feasible alternatives they

Seem to turn away from
a certain kind of life they
turn into something he couldn't

Understand something that
no longer writes even letters
all these so-called old friends

From school turn into some
thing he no longer bothers
calling when he gets to town

Morningland

Hasn't seen her
in years run into
her somewhere
south of LA she

Owns a health food
store is a member of
religious commune
something like that

Has friends named
karass and dharma
who wear airbrushed
t-shirts and order

Margaritas without
the tequila when we
go out for dinner
at the Mexican place

Cargo

Hotter than a pistol
or molten lead he
was so damn hot

Even angels' blood
would soon boil
as girls from cars

unload their cargo
of hot curves he
thought of Paris

Of being someone's
heir but all these
thoughts dropped

As he plunged
into cold water

Note To A Painter

I found it interesting
you labeled my
comments *pointless*

That same word
echoed here in this
early coffee morning

Book review perhaps
you are stuck I am not
even though I too have

Often found most things
pointless dull the knife
never sharp enough to

Pierce the skin but there
have been times when
the cut was so quick so

Deep a bold crimson
swatch splashed across
the page the taste

Incredibly sweet but
they were hard to see
you had to move quickly

To catch them had to listen
even when you knew there
was no point to filling in

The canvas which is what
I suppose John Thomas
was getting at when he

Noted the difference
between painters and
poets is that the latter

Do not have to keep
their hands still

Nevada

The myriad stars probably
sit out there a dotted line
stripe down a skunk's back

Or on a paved road the milky
way bobs like a canoe going
over the falls swept along by

The current too late to stop
only the moon comes up
like a grapefruit yellow yard

Light in the Nevada desert
coyote nuzzles the buck
hanging in the tree runs

Off when I open the
door to look for stars

Pecan Pies

It must have been
at least twenty five
years ago in a small

Texas town he'd sneak
into this old man's
backyard fill paper bags

With pecans he being
the youngest slower
than the rest was always

The one that got caught
had to stand there while
the old fool dumped his

Nuts on the ground and
stomped them now years
later on a shelf in Safeway

In a small Nevada town
there it is seems like the
first pecan pie he's seen

Since then even though
it's too much he buys it
takes it home cuts a slice

Finds only a few pecans
scattered here and there
on the top other than

Pecan pies and himself
which both seem a
little less the years have

Changed nothing really
out the window the same
cold wind whips up

Memories like dust devils
then blows on over a barren
landscape leaving nothing

Where once it seemed
there had been something

Going To The Post Office With My Son

Six times a week
he likes it yells
flag flag flag

When we get there
runs right on in while
I open the box dig it

Out he climbs the stairs
to those rarely visited
second floor offices sits

At the top waits for me
to ascend open the day's
catch lots of books and

Mags in there two checks
for $4.80 one acceptance
four rejection slips in there

While I read through them
he says hi to everyone
passing by underneath

Then we come down hand
in hand headed home for
the Sunday layover

Visitor

His knock rattles the door
so I get up let him in

Listening to him is like
getting stoned with a

Bunch of old friends
you haven't seen in

A long time you can
hear energy sound

Of lightning somewhere
in the air a bright flash

For a moment or two
but nothing really there

Through all that distance

Spiral

Watching Dick Clark
count toward the new
year in Times Square

Twenty below the baby
falls into the crowd
everybody cheering

Here it's the sound
of firecrackers one
or two quick rifle

Shots a little early
according to Dick's
countdown and it's

All over I switch off
the TV crawl under
the covers yard light

Outside coming
through the blinds
sound of a sonic

Boom cracking the
black Nevada night
like a nutshell spiraling

Away from me faster
and faster a dimly
remembered event

From my childhood
some toy broken so
many years ago

Dry Spell

The worst drought
in these here parts
old timers say in

Eighty-five years
then yesterday
more rain than

We've had all year
everything's flooded
buckets under holes

In the roof outside
the truck's stuck
in wet sand like

The words in my
head spinning
going nowhere

A Dark Night

I don't know why
cigarette smoke finds
the eye why I seem

To know no more
than the owl about
how or why the stars

Sit above me why I
sing like birds only
at sunrise or sunset

The points of change
of contact between
the light and the dark

Seem to be the ones
with the most interest
the ones to be looked

At understood that
certain things can
never be understood

Why we take the
chance is simply
beyond my grasp

Twinkling overhead
holding out a false
promise

Balm

On the way back from
the store a woman with
wine bottle empty

A gun in her purse
after a fight with her
old man who's still

In a nearby bar sat
down on the tracks
to rest in the heat

Which caused the
train to stop but
not soon enough

To prevent us from
being caught by
rail cars stretched

Across the intersection
in a string the fuse
that only has a certain

Number of years to
burn there is no balm
to heal such things

Monday Night Lovelock

Realize it's hard
to move on in the
desert but certain

Shortages force you
to try and understand
that things like drowning

In the desert sometimes
happen you drive around
look at the junk people let

Pile up around the house
as if somehow the sheer
accumulation of broken

Senseless sunbleached
things will fill the spaces
in their lives like the moon

Does the night wait till it
comes up listen to coyote
ask that cool yellow disc

For *relief* for *release* go back
to the motel switch on the
cooler swat a few mosquitos

Swirl the ice in your glass
settle down and watch the
Giants and Cubs slug it out

Without Apparent Cause

All of a sudden
things fall apart
without apparent

Or other cause slip
from your grasp
your palms not even

Wet as if you'd never
really held anything
at all things careen

Away from your control
are sucked back before
you know it you are

Two years old trying
to hold on to a piece
of bread while

Surrounded by four
barking dogs not
knowing you hold

The why the wherefore
right in your own hand
for a little while at least

Drumstick

I found a stick
that would do
a little longer

Than necessary
but you'll grow
scrounged up an

Old towel cut it
in three inch strips
covered them with

White buckskin
stitched that down
with waxed thread

Splitting the excess
for fringe cut more
fringe for the handle

Added brass tacks
two wing feathers
from a magpie and

It was done I hope
it gives you songs
that glide like a

Hawk out the kitchen
window all those clouds
and sky behind them

Badlands

It's the way things have
going nowhere running
dry hovering like a fly

No place to land finding
not what allured you in
that first pass only what

Threatens to remain with
out relief rattlesnake coiled
under a rock hungry and

Alone miles from water
the insensate blue of the
sky beats down buzzards

Circle the sun dry bed of
a river too long forgotten
these are indeed badlands

A flash flood would die of
thirst crossing these times

Adjusting To The Desert

Been getting dark earlier
light slipping away before
you notice winter comes

Cruising up to the dock
you wonder as you watch
the light fade just how the

Ship you've been expecting
can come in here where
even memories of the sea

Have long since dried up
and blown away
                                just then

Three stools down the moon
crosses her legs high lights a
cigarette and right at that

Moment you know what it
is coyotes keep asking for
she leaves early after driving

Everyone crazy with the sound
of her legs drinking up their
money making these promises

About how she'll show you so
much more tomorrow night
you listen to the broken-hearted

Cowboys on the jukebox
just so lonesome they could cry
while outside the stiff October

Wind tears at the petals of a
neon rose spinning everything
in sight like some nervous kid

His first time on a bar stool
after closing you stand on
the ditchbank think by not

Expecting a great deal or
believing too strongly in
things either too much or

Not enough here and
counting only on a dizzy
sense of well being you get

Under this totally irrational
sky that *shit* you just might
get by after all

I-80 Headed West

Coming down out of the Sierra
everything that bright new after
a rain growth green lady sitting

Beside me in the cab looking fine
short skirt riding up silken thighs
her hand on my knee some smoke

Cold beers passing round Merle
Haggard singing *White Line Fever*
on the KRAK country corral out

The windshield everything looking
good just oh so god damned good

NO DEPOSIT NO RETURN

I will be happy at the happy hour

—Gerald Locklin

I stood under the fortune palms
but all that came my way
was the remote echo of a woman's voice

—Tom Clark

Carpenteria

Full moon rising comes
in the open window
along with the sounds

Of a train hi-ballin' it
right on through this
small lemon packing

Town floats in the air
with the smell of *yesca*
from a gold metal flake

Buick Riviera cruising
this chick on the street
her black slit skirt

Flashing nylon leg
tonight on the self
proclaimed safest

Beach in the world
even the palms are
moving to the beat

Of her high heels on
the sidewalk the howl
of that southbound freight

South Laguna

There must be something
to be said for all of this

Blondes dressed in some
kind of hit me with your

Best shot mentality talking
from cocaine Porsche to

Burgundy Mercedes along
the cliffs as if the sun were

Their very own but at the
moment I'm damned if

I know what it could be

Apartment Living

Everyone's here being entertained
by big screen movies and tripping
from club to club by the notion

That this just might be where it's all
happening and the watery illusions
of leaving a room with four corners

Snapshots

He sometimes
noticed things
he was sure

Would take a
motor drive
Nikon high

Speed film
to catch but
when he looked

At them later all
he could see was
this old man

Snapping a shot
of hazy motionless
ocean and then

Quickly as if afraid
of being caught yet
somewhat reverently

Satisfied like he'd just
looked at a picture
of someone he hadn't

Seen in a long time
slip the Instamatic
into his hip pocket

Piracy

Limping home from a day
at the office Wallace Beery's
Long John Silver stopped at

The store was standing in
the express nine items or
less waiting to buy steak

Red wine when she walked
up arms laden with candy
for trick-or-treaters low cut

Black blouse tight orange
skirt black heels he saw him
self in a cocktail party room

Full of people where above
the collision of ice cubes the
muffled roar of conversation

He could hear the swish as
she crossed her legs saw her
look up quickly wondering

If anyone had noticed she
wished she wasn't standing
in line with caramels taffy

Peppermints wished she
wasn't buying this stuff
to sit home give it away

Wished she could get all
dressed up go somewhere
different maybe see from

Across a rum and coke filled
room someone watching her
walk across the parking lot

While a pirate skull and cross
bones moon rose above
her neon motel rendezvous

Rounding Third

—for Harry Reese

He noticed it walking
home from the store
a mushroom cloud

White about the size
of a golf ball he picked
it flipped it in the air

Two maybe three times
before he caught the glint
of the stream over there

Off to his left and turned
fired it into the breeze
like a rising second game

Of the series double that
takes off over the center
fielder's head he was

Digging hard for second
before he knew for sure
it would go and let up

Floated around third
watched it settle into
the creek easily surely

As if slapping the
obligatory after home
run hands still down

By one but feeling good
home safe with two bags
of groceries and a sixer

Listening To Hank Williams

In the bar she tells
him she could but
it's not what she

Wants in the store
she tells him she can't
try on everything

Or she won't get any
thing he pats a pint
of booze on his hip

Straightens his John
B. Stetson hat she
still feels the glow

From that shot back
in the bar balances
on a pair of wooden

Heels while he digs
the bills out of his
coat and pays she

Slips a black silk arm
through his under a
barely turning ceiling

Fan they walk out into
a dusty neon night with
only a quarter moon

For Now

She makes you
up a bed on the
floor of her all

Too frequently
otherwise occupied
gin and tonic eyes

In lieu of pouring
time from hand to
hand you fluff the

Pillow lie down it
doesn't really matter
it is enough for now

Years later she or
perhaps someone
who looks remarkably

Like her will say don't
you want to turn the
light out first and you

Trying to weigh the
cost wanting to see
just what it is will

Say as you reach
for her no no it
doesn't matter

It's okay for now
and it was and
it is for now

Fractions

She's a painter
recently split
from her old man

Also a painter she
tells him of some
note who's sold

Out found himself
a Santa Barbara lady
she speaks of living

Fast in the single lane
its drain on her work
how it's better with

A relationship that
works wants him to
come by the studio

Look at her paintings
especially this big
pink one that is

Somehow very erotic
the canvases are
rectangular divided

Into grids which she
fills with sections of
circles titles are fractions

Seven eighths
three quarters
nearly half

Things To Do At Jane's Cabin

Take a hike up the creek
look at trees as sculpture
check out the deeper pools

But don't see any fish split
wood find muscles you'd
forgotten break a mixing

Bowl wonder where you'll
find another catch up with
four weeks of mail lose

Interest watch pine needles
pile up on the truck wonder
how she got the place be

Damn glad she did find
what actually appears to
be bear shit in the woods

No Deposit No Return

He gets this note in the
mail lined notebook paper
a controlled feminine hand

I met you last week at the
Mermaid in Hermosa it
says do you remember she

Had strolled up smiled started
chatting about how she was
bored wanted to get out go

Somewhere different strange
she asked where he was from
so he gave her the numbers of

A place that hasn't been
kissed by the sea in a long
time it was enchanting she

Says she wanted neither
drink nor company took the
paper with his address he

Remembers watching her
walk away balanced on four
inch heels headed out the

Door into the setting sun the
tiny roses on her dress swaying
to and fro in the dim bar light

The note is signed with a big
lipsticked kiss but there's no
return address on the envelope

HINDSIGHT

you can never not look back

—Terry Allen

you can't escape gravity

—Captain Beefheart

The Photograph

It is probably somewhere
in the Pacific Northwest
the wallpaper appears

Damp looks like it has
been for years soft wet
mildewed the colors

Running like someone's
long forgotten sheets
there is an old dresser

Placed diagonally across
the corner of the room
it is probably oak but

Painted over badly chipped
with four pedestals and
the center all covered with

Clean white doilies on each
pedestal there is a small jar
with some kind of flowers

That don't grow anywhere
around here and in the
front right hand corner

A kerosene lantern there
are probably other objects
in the room but my eyes

Aren't as good as they
once were I can no longer
make them out and it

Was taken so long
ago I cannot *remember*
what they were

On The Dresser

Beginning to yellow
and curl stuck in
the lower right

Hand corner of
the mirror a small
fading kodachrome

Of an attractive
young redhead
probably So-Cal

In the '50s posed
on a car fender her
legs are crossed

So high you can
see the metallic
sheen of her black

Satin slip is a much
deeper black than
the palm tree

Shadows on that
white stucco wall
behind the large

Silver hoops which
tug heavily on
her pierced ears

Mason Lake

Dull gray winter days
water penetrates to the
bone infecting everything

With a dampness that
never dries all day
fussing with firewood

So wet it does little other
than smoke and sizzle
the neighbor's boat has

Filled and sunk my son
goes out to give the ducks
some bread I try to free

A coffee cup from the
mountain of unwashed
dishes the Franklin stove

Sounds like a steam plant
and outside even the ducks
are beginning to complain

Something No One Catches

I know something
I'd like to tell you
but you don't want

To listen don't want
to hear what I have
to say but wait listen

Although the rain
cleared the sunset
was troublesome

Like never knowing
what to say to someone
who asks how you've

Been it was as small
distant and red as
the eyes you pass

In cattle trucks on
a late night highway
their breath steaming

Into the air through
little round holes and
after it was gone it

Was so still I could hear
fish jump clean on the
other side of the lake

Exactly Eight Degrees

Six to eight small rounds
maple that's been down
for bout a year sposed to

Be dry but still smokes
sizzles when split and
burned in a Franklin stove

For seven hours say from
eight to three on a rainy
Saturday will in the course

Of that time raise the
temperature of the house
exactly eight degrees

When It Will Happen

Sometime perhaps
by accident as if
finding a forgotten

Note hidden in your
stockings and lingerie
sometime perhaps

For no apparent
reason at all while
walking past a store

Window admiring
your reflection or
some morning putting

On your makeup
sometime perhaps
a long time from

Now after I'm gone
it will happen I am
sure of it you'll think

Of me the brief smile
at the memory of us
will fall from your

Hand as you burst
into tears and as
it shatters right there

In front of you
you'll realize what
you should have known

Finally see what you
should have fucking seen
so very long ago

Edges

I.

Sitting in front of the fire
trying to stay warm
lonesome songs in his

Radio thinking about maybe
taking a ride all the way
down to where palm trees

Live watching it start to get
dark fog begin to form out
over the lake wondering

Why no matter how bright
the water doesn't reflect
the much written about

Stars above can't light
the dark below like a
fool his radio says

To want to ride on a train
when the trains is all gone

II.

Socked in for four
days pea soup so
thick the dock just

Twenty feet outside
his window shoved
off never to be seen

Again but today for
a moment just for
a moment a pale

White sun almost
burned through
there was a minute

Of blue sky the lake
tried to crawl from
inky gray toward

Green the dock was
sighted steaming
toward shore then

It came swirling back
nearby things couldn't
hold their edges grew

Soft went out of focus
began to fade like the
memory of a totally

Pleasant day from his
own not too distant past

Rheumatoid Variants

He cannot move
from in front of the
stove even forgets

About chasing the
few winter flies that
have made it in out

Of the cold from his
brow his son tells
him it's important

To know where the
flies go he doesn't
know what happens

To them but like
them he is
thankful just to

Be able to move
around is some kind
of minor miracle

A few new poems palm
trees on the glass around
three fingers of rum

Hindsight

Greener pastures in time turn
to indian summer brown severe
fire danger hills which go up in

Smoke and then under constant
driving rain with nothing to hold
it slide right through your fingers

WEST NEVADA WALTZ

she hung the moon but she hung it upside down

—George Jones

the tune is cowboy, the words sentimental crap
farther out the wind is mending sagebrush

—James Welch

Mustard Colored Rain

Going back retracing your
steps looking for something
you've lost something you

Had at least thought you did
once in the only theatre of
a small Nevada town you

Watch the film begin to run
crazily back toward its can
it's old badly scratched hard

To see through what appears
to be mustard colored rain
you cannot see *exactly* what

What was going on back there
but it's where you must have
lost something you need now

The keys to unlock your door
heat the early morning dark so
you squint and keep on looking

The Misfits

Clark and Marilyn are
sitting in a bar in Reno
drinking doubles talking

About leaving not to any
place in particular just
moving on getting out

The jukebox is spouting
something about hanging
in and hanging on like

Autumn leaves before they
fall it was true it would be
an early winter for although

There were few trees to shed
their leaves the honkers were
already heading south and it

Was only the twenty-third
of August they could barely
hear the music above the

Dull mechanical roar of the
casino a combination of silver
dollars dropped into slots

Handles being pulled and
bells going off every time
someone put in three and

Got two back there were
old women sitting on red
naugahyde stools pulling

The handles again and again
with a slow desperate assembly
line familiarity as if they'd sat

On those same stools for twenty
five years *You know* she says *I*
walked out to the city limits once

It didn't look like much was out there
Clark kills his drink in one gulp
motions to the bartender to bring

Them another round nods at her
and says *yeah but it may be*
the only place there's anything left

They look at one another
across the table and something
passes between them like

A sudden breeze across the
furnace of a Nevada afternoon
they leave the bar find his

Battered pickup drive up
Virginia to fourth street then
head east into the desert

Leaving Reno and a technicolor
even in black and white
sunset behind them

Looking At Maps

The Great Basin least
spectacular of all
North American deserts

Almost the entire state
contained within its
boundaries where

What would barely
pass elsewhere for
a stream is a river

And none of them
will ever find the sea
even so we have less

Water and more desert
around us than anywhere
else including Arizona the

County had more than
seventy towns come but
because the ore played

Out fire burned them
or water dried up only
Fallon continued to grow

Today the eastern
county line is not
known exactly and

The western edge of town
reaches toward Reno
saying Raley's Sprouse

Rietz Country Kitchen
Kentucky Fried Chicken but
if you look at the old maps

And listen you'll hear

Bango *Bolivia*
Bell Flat *Bunejug Mountains*

Carson Sink *Cocoon Mountains*
Dixie Valley *Dead Camel Mountains*

Eastgate *Eightmile Flat*
Forty Mile Desert *Frenchman's*

Hard To Find *Hazen*
Ione *Job's Peak*

La Plata *Middlegate*
Mirage *Mopung Hills*

Quicksilver *Ragtown*
Salt Wells *Sand Mountain*

Seeho Springs *Stillwater*
Stinking Springs *Swingle Bench*

Westgate *White House Rock*
Wildcat Station *Wonder*

Yomba

Finding Stillwater

It's really not that hard
to find although many
have passed by few

Stopped fewer yet stayed
not even the county seat
remained for long it's not

That everything you need
will be here it's that so
much you don't will not

Be so bring what you cannot
give up wanting with you
think of it as a place you're

Always it seems either coming
from or going to it's not that
far from where you are right

Now calling probably from
a bar uptown although it
sometimes looks out the

Window an awfully lot like
it feels inside your head
before you adjust your

Margins put the paper in
right now there are clouds
the color of the light in the

Center of a glass of white
wine floating around on
the faded blue levis of the sky

Mirage Factor

There are several things
about weather around
here you can more or

Less count on among
them heat cold and
wind it's rare to draw

Three at once but a pair
is not unusual adding
to the wind you draw

One of those winter come
back in late March days
on which you have to

Go into Reno on business
it's somewhere around
Mustang or Painted Rock

With it gusting at seventy
or eighty miles an hour
there's an eighteen wheeler

Jack-knifed on the interstate
and the truck's heater going
full tilt can't hold off

The cold that you realize
you've been here *right here*
before the feeling strikes

Suddenly as they say
without warning you see
coming home through dust

And tumbleweeds the inverted
reflections of distant things
grow closer last fall's leaves

Are sucked up to float
around and around
in front of you then

Although lightning's
not supposed to
twice you watch

The sun in your rearview
drop into what you
distinctly remember as

The humming mosquito
colored air of a late
last July afternoon

Ten Gallon Clouds

It's after midnight
for the first time
since seven this

Morning you switch
the cooler off just
five minutes ago

You're sweating
already what's left
of the moon finally

Comes up too hot
to sleep you turn
on the one channel

You get out here
John Wayne's lawless
frontier is all there is

110° today hotter
tomorrow the forecast
calls for *some* clouds

In the afternoon
you'll probably even
wish for rain just to

Cool things down but
know it will not come
know that you have

To wait it out as the
ichthyosaurs did
drying up with the

Sea here where dark
and light collide under
the blankets of the sky

Reflections In A Desert Wind

The mirror is chipped
pitted the surface almost
worn away from constant

Battering of driven sand
the images look as if they've
been there a long time but

Appear suddenly like
middle age the onset
of arthritis at thirty-two

Or a desert wind on a 99°
day you can actually
see it moving toward

You at first it doesn't
look like it will be *that*
bad the climate after all

Is supposed to be good
for it then you see from
seventy miles away a twelve

Foot woman on fire a man
on trial for shooting his
four month old son

Finally its strength is too
much the saplings have
all bent double everything

Is layered with fine dust
you watch tumbleweeds
let go roll with the rippling

Metal sound single wides
make on such a day for
a while you're moving

Along fairly well but
any sudden intrusion
or marshaling of the facts

Even small ones stretched
thin and taut as wire
between fenceposts hangs

You up stops you are stuck
there so long even the
smallest amount of effort

Becomes too much though
you can still hear it coming
from some distance off

The by now only half
remembered song of her
wind blown hair moving

Across the desert's face
so you listen but no longer
know if this is the right place

Or if like holding a door or a
coat it's just a matter of being
there at the right time look

Even the curtains are dancing
straight out in the air
almost parallel to the floor

Fallon

You've driven over
nine hundred miles
just to be here for a

Few days where it's
warm enough dry
enough to sit on

The porch in the
sun on a day after
Christmas under

A sky you'd almost
forgotten could be
so blue the few

Clouds are so high
and thin that when
they pass in front

Of the sun there's no
change in the light
and it takes a while

For you to feel your
shirt growing cold
against your skin

But the chill passes
quickly like a first
snow that sticks

Around only in the
shadows of the
ditchbank so you

Decide to walk up get
the mail with the sky
the only coat around you

Distance

Moving away it takes
a while for things you
thought lost to reappear

Sooner or later they do and
you find the differences
are not ones of contrast

But the lack of it gone
are salt white clouds
and deep azure sky

There things were more
diffuse less certain a TV
set with no contrast

Everything was gray
muted once you left
the desert's heat to sit

In front of a wood stove
most of the day trying
to decide which was

The right piece to burn
next which would catch
not fill the house with

Smoke while through
your window you watched
greens blues even the blacks

Of a moonless night bleed
into gray under constant
billowing rain after five

Straight days it finally let
up and became so foggy
that even though the softest

Sounds were amplified they
remained as distant as the worn
out feelings of an old record

Seeing The Light

Warm under late afternoon
mid-February bright blue sky
salsa in the kitchen window

Full of immense blue backed
flat bottomed white clouds
floating by honky tonks and

Harsh lights on your radio
the air is as crisp as the light
you can see it coming for

Miles and miles sneaking
in and out of the clouds
as if looking for someplace

Better safer to stash the loot
and finding no place better
than right here

West Nevada Waltz

I learned how to listen for
a sound like the sun going down
—Rodney Crowell

It isn't so much a matter
of not looking a gift horse
in the mouth but rather

A matter of not looking
any horse in the mouth
out here valleys are

Measured in miles across
and no matter how long
it takes out there in the

Middle under the sun
you like fall always seem
to arrive just barely in time

After a while there's no
longer enough left to
waste on crossing the

Damn things just to see
if it's any better over there
after all are folks who've

Pretty much decided the
same thing somewhere
along the line even though

There are those times when
like a horse tethered in one
place too long you reach

The end of your rope you
begin to settle in begin to
forget the *cherry cherry orange*

Combinations which didn't
pay off and noticing only
how easily the bright yellow

Leaves all around this so
called oasis let go start to
waltz toward the ground

You believing she just might
show up again begin to wait
for the moon which like an

Expected check always takes
too long shows up late
stumbling across the black ice

Of the sky like a tipsy redhead
in high heels full but still in the
1981s only worth a quarter she's

Not much what with her makeup
smeared and all often looking
the next day like noontime neon

Showing only a hint of what
she was the night before but
right now up there shimmering

Almost dancing across that
nimble three-quarter time blue
sky she looks like the damndest

Schooner you ever did see and
of course there are the clouds

PAINTING

landscape is character not background

—Walter Van Tilburg Clark

location is both a geographic term
and an inner sense of being

—Robert Creeley

Coffee

He put the water on
sat with country roads
on the radio bits and

Pieces of poems flung
about trying to figure
or at least remember

Trying to make a cup
some sense out of
something wasn't

Moving like he used
to kept stumbling
over what he should

Be stepping on he stood
at the window thinking
how nice it might be

Someone to rub his neck
he watched the wind swirl
dusty bourbon air heard

Sudden slap of wooden
screen door times here
weren't so good but

Really not so bad either
he ground his own
beans drank it black

Moments

You sit there try
to remember when

That was just how
long ago you saw

Yourself in this or
that sepia yellowed

Snapshot memory
standing there

Holding nothing
as if it were a fish

The Color Of Water

—for Jess

Around here the wind
rolls with no particular
destination moves like

A knife toward its target
until exhausted by the
attempt it stretches out

Tries to hold onto the
color of water which
is of course the same

As those naked trees madly
waving in answer to
questions yet to be asked

Frisbee

—for Cody

Lemon moon no sky
above an orange chair
a man disappeared

Last time it was full
clouds no bigger
than nickels begin

To work their way
across the sky
miraculous as slugs

In a Nevada bathroom
it is here the so-called
moral of the story

Begins to fly across
the lawn while the
rest of the barely

Visible light rages
behind indigo peaks

The Dentist

Your teeth begin to
look juvenile almost
incandescent more

And more vacant after
twenty-three brushings
they're glass the stuccoed

Druggist sings looney
tunes to replace your
mouth's verdant acids

With polypeptide chains
speaks well of the
penultimate artist

Who stimulates women
under a probably only one
of its kind true blue sky

How It Is

It is colder than anyone
around here can remember
it ever getting rain turns to

Snow covers the alkali and
saltgrass for two weeks the
usually bluer than anyplace

Else sky is the color of a day
time moon a neon wind pulls
the color from everything

Even the sage then it clears
off temperatures *really* drop
pipes freeze tree limbs snap

Break you buy another
kerosene heater close off
rooms scrape ice from the

Inside of kitchen windows
you wait for better days
read old poems know that

You are no longer young
enough to be coy about it
things really weren't any

Better back then back *there*
but there were a few bright
moments poems caught here

And there like dew in a web
finally it begins to thaw
things come back things you've

Forgotten come popping up
through the snow even the
moon is back in the black

The snow's melting off
you're drunk on the coming
through the window sun

Hitting your back haven't yet
realized tomorrow will be
nothing but mud it is like

Love which more than any
thing else is those few bright
moments in between

Straws

How can you explain
what 3:30 will bring
I know it will probably

Be late but try and be
as precise as you can
where will the hands

Be what will they be
doing holding a brush
a book of poems or

Grasping at straws it's
hard to tell tentative as
they are not wanting to

Put that final one
on the camel's back

Bad Roads

It snowed the day
he left she stood

At the window
watched flakes

Fill the muddy ruts
of his tire tracks

Postcard From Nowhere

The beer's expensive
but good radio full
of cracked dreams

Lost wishes things
look pretty much
the same as every

Where else and by
nightfall he's flat
out on his back

Blue Basin

Looks good on
the surface cool
if you're hot still

Moving if you're
frozen stiff but go
below that carefully

Polished ready to
present to the public
surface and it gets

Messy slippery hard
to hang onto the dark
secrets of hidden

Boulders spots so deep
all light all sense of
direction even the ability

To move is lost you realize
it too late try to call out
above the roar of clouds

Receding dancing around
and finally down the great
blue basin of the sky

Tahoe

Out on the deck astride
a certain point of the after
noon there is not much

Noise an occasional voice
drifting up from the lake
soto voce of Chopin's piano

Clouds boil over the ridge
to the west stretch thin
white talons toward his

Chardonnay and some
thing perhaps the sky's
envy of *that* blue causes

The wind to begin to move
slowly at first the notes
from a flute begin to lift

The edges of the water

All Day Long

The air has been choked
thick with yellow dust
swirling like some angry

Top around the basin
finally late afternoon
the clogged faucet clears

Rain begins and it looks
as if it's hailing the manic
yellow ochre of a Van Gogh

Billboard peeling there on
an afternoon in between cloud
bursts sun struck wheatfield

Punctuation

Lust colored hair that
when properly punctuated
by rain wrestling in the

Liquid air sounds as if
it could be mighty fine
indeed to be tangled there

Tomatoes

Beefsteak roma or pear
shape is everything

There is of course
the color of their legs

Against that
yellow bus bench.

Potatoes

New ones
are prized
even desired

Small ones
are not

Gray

Rain for a week he left
no note had been seen
walking by the river

Thirty minutes before
but it probably looked
too cold and he retreated

Back into a short dog of
white port then climbed
six flights of stairs after

Not being able to quite
figure out the elevator
walked once around the

Rim where he could not
equal as it may have
been find even the

Smallest patch of blue

One Deep Breath

Deceptive as the sun
breaking through fifteen
ice every morning till noon

Days beautiful for a while
but soon growing dreary
two pots of coffee by ten

Watching for that package
the one that should arrive
today and with one deep

Breath highlight a landscape
the luminists would have loved

A Body Of Work

He started counting
he did not know
exactly where to begin

But he began keeping
this discarding that
counting only the former

Later some of the latter
became as attractive as
a diamond shaped sign

Looming suddenly up
out of the fog just in time
to lean into the curve

Without breaking the
thought he was trying
so hard to hang onto

Delivering The Show

Frain across the state
for nine days no one
in the valleys has seen

The sun those who've
left only when they
hit the summit where

Briefly the landscape
is equal parts Nepal
and Diebenkorn before

Slipping back down into
sixty miles of tule fog

Approaching Valmy

The song your threadbare
tires sing to the asphalt
at three A.M. just fourteen

Miles out of Valmy Nevada
with now even the Great Salt
Lake airborne and drifting off

Into the rearview

Battle Mountain

Valley fog lifts
only over the pass
air so heavy

In the Owl Club
he could not stay

Tonopah

Sunday twenty degrees
she's buying a twelve pack
digging in her parka for

Change rocking back
and forth in red pumps
chattering on and on

And on about how
it could be worse
how it could be

For Christ's sake
Butte

Embers

The light has changed
crystallized into cold
bands of hazy yet

Intense color mountains
to the east glow like
stubborn wood hanging

Onto what is left of the
light huddled around
the embers of a dark

Line drawn by the night
two days into November

Gossip

The wind is whispering
among last month's
stripped clean branches

Trying to stir something
up pushing fallen leaves
across the sand swirling

Here and there into the
blunt semaphore of a
wavering twilight

Spreading small smudges
the color of fire and ice
across the lip of the sky

GETTING ACROSS

the signs say KEEP MOVING
—Richard Shelton

After leaving the confused
footsteps of a neon twilight
behind and driving out

Here you begin taking it
apart watching piece by
high gloss enamel piece

Fade and peel in the desert
sun until a fine white
powder falls from tubes

That can no longer remember
the hum and buzz of color
you look at everything

Closely shift it slightly as
if hoping that sudden
play of light will lend it

More than it has to offer
the words you thought
so right have begun to

Sound like sand in the
margins of a place
no one dares to cross

Everywhere around
the edges shards of
broken amber glass

Saying *you are not*
the first to think about
trying it here

Sirocco

Outside the wind is busy
sanding everything down
to only what must remain

And with chapped senseless
lips stands there muttering
of what it could have been

Painting

I feel as if I am
too near the sky
all the time
—Marsden Hartley

The mountains appeared
to be right there at the end
of this road but he knew

They were close to maybe
a hundred miles off he
was sitting on the lawn

Thinking about a figure
ground relationship that
would hold together

Work even when looked
at closely for a long time
sooner or later he like

The leaves would know
it was time and when he
did as much from necessity

As choice he'd have to go
have to move again like
clouds just can't keep still

Changing from one thing
to another right before his
eyes the cool September

Afternoon grass of his child
hood where he watched
biplanes form letters

Overhead began to itch
and the skywriting came
apart with a horrible

Cracking sound that ended
up hanging there for years
like some bad motel room

Painting just above his
line of vision it was a land
scape into which winter

Came sooner than expected
outside trees with half
their leaves still on broke

Under the strain the birds
he thought he had in his
hands pulled together into

A raggedy pink flock
and headed south the
brief purple orange rush

Of joy on the mountains
gradually turning gray
before it was gone

DRIVING TO VEGAS

empty agenda on a full tank
that's the way to go

—Jeanette Robertson

the image of cherries
on a slot machine
is far from innocent

—Amy Spindler

Waiting

For an answer to
your letter the pitcher
to make his move

Toward the plate for
the proofs to come
back from the printer

Waiting in lines banks
grocery stores the post
office waiting out the

Rain for the sun to
go down the moon
to come up waiting

For the paint to dry
for the leaves to fall
the fever to break

For the check to
arrive your lover
your wife to turn

Toward you with
a smile waiting
for the wind to

Lift a skirt waiting
for the world to
wake up and notice

Brake Lights

Sometimes if I can
find it I look at the
map how far it is

From here to there
we're all different
tend to end up I

Suppose where
it's best but still
we yearn to get

From here to there
others impatient
with all this distance

Make these roads
bright brake lights
strung along the

Cloudless interstate
great basin night

Four Or Five Beers
Dorsey's Bar
Gabbs Nevada

Don't know why
I came out here

Circumstances
I guess

Weren't no woman
or the law

Probably just cuz the
wheel didn't turn right

And you know I've left
more'n a few times

But after a while I start
to feel like ice must

As it freezes and I
end up comin' back

You know I can't complain
if I get rained on

I know it ain't
no picture show

Withered

Shot through
tattered

An old target on
a bale gone gray

Hairlines

Always the cracks
you cannot see

Hairlines between
cerulean and crimson

Leading somewhere
the only way out

Back how you came

Outside Ely In The Rain

Bleary-eyed four
A.M. café your breath
floating in front of you

Suddenly catches the
sound of a fan back
and forth the crackles

Of red neon push through
the rain across a damp gray
field stinking of sage

Not Quite Dark

Still over eighty
driving home
twenty watt bulbs

Of bathrooms adrift
in alfalfa begin to
throw their rays

Of hope up into
the leaving indigo
turning oh so quickly

To mars black sky
which now appears
to be running right

Alongside the car
your hand's out the
window knitting

Feeble white dots
together as it floats
along feeling the

Air squeeze its flesh
like some not quite
ready avocado

Sifting

Wood screws loose
in a drawer too many
different sizes no two

Alike all too short
to hold it together
all of them for one

Reason or another
somehow worth
saving

It's Not As If Everything Came From New York

It's as if we're crossing
this river on foot the
current stronger

Than we thought
we step cautiously
into still spots tell

Ourselves to think
about depth think
instead about getting

Burned while we
are swept away

Incidental Music

A dark gray front
moves impulses
around the sky

My potatoes boil
in a pot the fridge
hums with desperate

Certainty the leaves
after being green for
so long yellow and fall

Schwitters

Hearing the rain break up in syllables
—Pamela Stewart

Early but never early
enough I come to shave
the idea of my face in

The morning mirror
if only I knew where
everything is supposed

To be that is impossible
but something is near
and I can hear the rain

Breaking up in syllables
speaking slowly trying
out a new tongue one

Nearly as fluid as when
love is new and things
fall together like scraps

In a Schwitters collage
of crumpled blue sky
I keep looking out

The window wondering
just where you are right
now nothing is as

Innocent or unconnected
as we once so naively
thought in the cabinet

Six separate bottles
all saying pain

Seurat

The disappearance of
days accelerated came
to be measured solely

By the mail the day
the date being replaced
this year by another

Beginning amid the
drone of last year's
bloated promises

Cast ashore thrown
so far above high tide
line the cartridges are

Jammed into the
chambers and spun
like shattered

Fragments of the sky
into a bitterly
pointillistic notion

That it was all probably
due to things best not
spoken of no not here

Two Step

She's short dark but
looks pale in the almost
purple motel light

Talks about possibilities
about dancing a two-step
across the wreck of the west

He begins to think twice
the same thought blinking
on and off above the cars

Huddled in the dubious lot

Pollock

Look closely you'll begin
to see splattered chrome
bumper reflections a

Turquoise '59 El Camino
in the parking lot slick
with rain smell of wet

Asphalt her fugitive scent
and wind whipped hair
nothing nothing at all

Under those madly
waving colors

Rothko

Hanging on here
is it that way there
too the early March

Afternoon clock
ticking one more
one less pacing

Back and forth
if you want you
can perhaps change

You don't think
that's enough but
look the smoke

From my cigarette
always rises takes
your eyes away

From the ice
as it melts
in your glass

Trapped here
under the lust
and closed air

Of a compressed
Rothko sky

Hopper

An off-white tempera
afternoon in a would
be chrome diner the

Sun attempts to pour
meaning into what is
best seen at closing time

Last night the slit ebony
cloth of the sky revealed
the cross legged flesh

Of the moon high heels
hooked on the rung of
a stool hanging on in

Trembling bar sign light

Arts Administration

In the bar we wonder
why we bother to
continue the trying

To find a place for
the artist ending up
taking all of art's time

Twilight In San Juan

Hornitos blue jeans and
neon back of the bar
reminded him of the

Sound of her heels moving
down the hallway of that
cheap hotel in San Juan

Stopping in front of 214
to retrieve something that
tumbled out of her hastily

Packed bag she lit a cigarette
before moving on down the
cadmium splashed walls

Without once looking back

RNO - LAX

Over an hour late
fog at SFO the excuse
for another drink

After lunch with
Heizer scale is
the issue time the

Question distance
the difference if
you're on the left

You've got a nice
view of the city on
the right unspeakable

Blackness of the Pacific
flight attendant makes
last pass for glasses

Small bells in her ears
hard eyes he remembered
the color of her stockings

Same as Michael's earth
toned cement and the
less than half dollar

Sized moon dropping
off to the left as they
descended into a sea

Of lights that punishes
the limits of our vision

Fog At The Borders Of The Palms

The discordant music of
the twentieth century
is small recompense

For a mist that thickens
the air conducts the wind
and a light so horrible

It could neither note any
music nor guide us
through the daily accident

As we lean into each
other in an unmade room

Drawing To An Inside Straight

Dust swirls behind
you down Indian
Lakes road almost

There you tell yourself
no longer sure why
you're going what will

Happen when you get
there fish and white
pelicans do you remember

The time your son slipped
under gagging spitting as
he broke the surface glad

To see the sky the time
you came on a picnic
today there's nothing

Only what the wind
left behind muttering
in the trees

Yeah, yeah
shut up and deal

Driving To Vegas

Tonopah's the place
contour lines appear
to rise between there

And Goldfield the first
joshua trees beer at the
Mozart Club from then

On it's all downhill
between Mercury
and Indian Springs

The light begins to
change you wonder
what you'll do when

You reach the edge
of the map out there
on the horizon all

That neon beckoning
you in from the dark

RED WEB

the hardest thing to learn
is which bridge to cross
and which to burn

—David Russell

in the desert failure has
unmistakable force very
little blocks the view

—Charles Bowden

The Opening

—for Walter McNamara

Every year or so whatever
it is you've been trying to
figure out at whatever point

It's gotten to is packed up
carted off hung somewhere
for a month maybe six weeks

That first night people you've
never seen maybe met once
somewhere show up briefly

It's nice watching the social
swirl in front of your work
cheap white wine for anyone

Who holds out their plastic
cup three hours it's all over
except for lame reviews in

Sunday's paper which will
miss the point if not totally
then at least completely

Fishin' In The Dark

—a song for Michael Sarich

I.

Wonder why I think too
much expanding explodes
what I just convinced my

Self was there to think I
can be strong or over matter
is bullshit attempting meaning

Thinking makes me thirsty
I try to forget all I've over
estimated don't really know

Who I am what I'm supposed
to be which one is me under
this not so carefully polished

Surface try and hold on to what
I see but everywhere I look
sideways and around honesty

Is dissolving before it reaches
the edge I'd much rather float
around safe in senseless blue

Touch fear pain seem to make
things real if you can touch
them if you can if it goes

This far if you can feel it
it's real the senseless
mumblings of pure touch

II.

Juggling what's good what's
bad why we always get hit
here a closely stoppered vial

Rattling around in an open
and shut case it's always
too close then too far touch

And fear striped open hungry
mouths on a barber pole why
do we always get hit here

Touch fear pain seem to make
things real if you can touch
them if you can if it goes

This far if you can feel it
it's real the senseless
mumblings of pure touch

III.

The real heart the real head
has to take it from the other
two has to feel it when they

Open when they close their
god damn fish tail hands
trying to hold me in place

But still it comes to the
surface and you know
that if you feel it it's true

Touch fear pain seem to make
things real if you can touch
them if you can if it goes

This far if you can feel it
it's real the senseless
mumblings of pure touch

IV.

Don't care what they all say
I hear more than you think
it ends up here where things

Really get polished after all
that philosophical moaning
it's simply biological after all

It's what I'm supposed to do
greatness and stupidity
wrapped up in one

Touch fear pain seem to make
things real if you can touch
them if you can if it goes

This far if you can feel it
it's real the senseless
mumblings of pure touch

Artists' Statements

Aesthetics is for artists
like ornithology is for
birds an object never

Serves the same function
as its image or its name
take an object do something

To it do something else to it
do something else to it I only
know my materials to what

End I know not it doesn't
have anything to do with
materials or style it's a kind

Of energy that comes into
the particular sequence
of events art is a marriage

Of the conscious and the
unconscious art disease
is caused by a hardening

Of the categories it's more
important to be in the theatre
than it is to know what's

Going on in the movie
living in the desert has
taught me to go inside

Myself for shade without
music life would be a
mistake a writer is not

So much someone
who has something
to say as he is someone

Who has found a process
that will bring about new
things he would not have

Thought of if he had not
started to say them I have
nothing to say and I am

Saying it and that is poetry
poetry is always a dying
language but never a dead

Language the grass is always
greener on the other side of
the fence but it's just as hard

To cut few understand how
past and over the past is
language or the absence of it

Is extremely critical for the
conceptualization of imagery
when critics get together they

Talk about form and space
when painters get together
they talk about turpentine

Talking about art is like
trying to french kiss
over the telephone

Barnett Newman • Rene Magritte • Jasper Johns
Kurt Schwitters • William T. Wiley • Jean Cocteau
Ad Reinhardt • David Byrne • Richard Shelton
Frederich Nietzsche • William Stafford • John Cage
Robert Smithson • Little Richard • Donald Kuspit
Pablo Picasso • Terry Allen

Rim To Rim

Just the smell hay under
a quarter moon pushes
toward you just the clouds

In early light trying to mimic
her hair just an empty hanger
the crickets keep calling for

Just the leaves calling you
to the door just watching
darkness give up more

Than you thought possible
but look the sun has begun
to crawl over the Stillwaters

And now rim to rim the sky
is streaked with red tendrils
moving moving in your mind

Personal Values, 1952

It was mid-afternoon he
was still out in the studio
painting she lit some candles

Took a hot bath lingered
drinking campari and soda
until the water cooled she

Shaved her legs got out of
the tub sat on the hamper
pulled on her stockings

Enjoying feel of the silk as
she walked into the bed
room pausing to pull back

And tie the white lace
curtains outside fluffy
white clouds skidded

Around the corners of
the sky she decided on
the black dress *quelle*

Suprise the one he'd
bought her in Brussels
and a black pearl choker

It probably didn't matter
what he always noticed
was her legs and shoes

He'd even done a painting
a very sexy painting
of them was the only one

To pay attention to how
she dressed she liked that
she loved his mind how

He infused everything
even watching her eat
raspberries and ice cream

With some kind of off the
wall symbolic resonance
she was supposed to meet

Him at 5:30 but didn't feel
like going she wasn't sure
why recent events objects

Associated with them
seemed to have grown
larger to occupy more

Of her thoughts than she'd
like and decided she really
wasn't feeling that well

After all perhaps lunch
had been a bit too spicy
she was suddenly very

Tired but decided against
lying down she felt
exposed as if outdoors

Half naked on a windy
day besides the bed
looked entirely too small

To be comfortable to get
ready she had to dig
through the wardrobe

Try and find the dress
decide on which shoes
when she passed the

Wardrobe she liked
what the mirror saw
she had hennaed her

Hair and although
right now the thought
of having to comb

The snarls out was
unbearable she knew
it would all be worth it

Driving To Montana With V

—for Bill Kittredge

Anaconda Gillette Goldfield
Havre Sheridan Winnemucca
so many others seems you

Always come in against the
wind with just the right light
inside which you hear the

Ripple of trailer tops squatting
on the edge of town most have
given up all hope of ever seeing

Rubber again jealous of so-called
mobile homes that have never
seen it a little farther in sheet

Metal shop buildings have tried
to settle only to become flaking
in the sun WW II quonset huts

Closer to the center western stores
red brick neon bars the *places* of
those that tried it here first all

Of them all of them trying to
remember over five or six
beers in the center of a hazy

Valley floor what they felt
like the first time they saw
those mountain peaks break

The windy aluminum colored sky

School

Her red nails
scratching

The blackboard
of his heart

Out Here

On the antennae
of what we feel

My hands
on this page

Only to feel
you on the

Other side of
these words

Distant Coyotes

You hear the sound
for miles and miles

Wind howling from
the heart when it feels

Passion's deposition
being taken elsewhere

Looking

Someone with your hair
didn't have your eyes
someone with your eyes

Didn't have your smile
someone with your smile
didn't have your legs

Someone with your legs
didn't have your spirit
someone with your spirit

Didn't have my heart
it's been out driving
all night long across

The desert's face
looking looking
looking for you

Poetry

Like gardening
or painting
is a process

Liking what
you see until
finally you see

What you like

At Workman's

Spring almost Easter
walking amidst brightly
growing things offers

Solace from the days
reminds him of last year
her words then as now

Stargazer lilies whisper
love without clocks
overwintered bleeding

Hearts speak of having
dinner by the flickering
candlelight of how

It's getting better

Driving God And The Grieving Widow

It starts out with who
done what to whom
soon becomes lit-crit

Poetry and the novel
having a family dispute
the canine novelist peeing

On everything in sight
while the feline poet
sneaks next door

Eats the neighbor's food

Exquisite

Beautiful as in her
big-mouthed high
heeled grin purpose

Fully striding across
the room also intense
as in bone pain

Heartbreak

Candle

Clouds sliding over
the Sierra as he came
around the bend

Reminded him a black
pleated skirt that grin
under hooded eyes

Swinging her legs
high into the truck
hand on the back

Of his neck the
unexpected candle
suddenly lit

Dust

Coalesces in autumn air
wraps me in her hand
rain on October fields

Austin to San Antonio
her skin pale as love's
first evening star in a

Room high above
the Rio Colorado

Fado For A Sultry Afternoon With The Blinds Partly Pulled

A beachfront motel
just across the tracks
from the beach a hot

Sultry afternoon red
splash of bougainvillea
limp from the heat

Trailing on the balcony
railing palm trees are
motionless even the ocean

Seems too tired to make
waves of any sort blinds
are partly pulled a shaft

Of sunlight streams
across the room to her
auburn hair what're you

Thinking she asks he'd
been sitting there trying
to come up with a title

For a book of poems
nothing was coming oh
nothing he replies sets

Down his glass looks up
she has on a short black
silk dress is straightening

Her seams she walks
toward him heels clicking
across the tile floor dress

Rustling in the pellucid
air as she perches on
the edge of a chair crosses

Her legs sips bubbles from
her flute don't worry about
it baby she says it'll come

Red Web

Mid-afternoon she sleeps
in the intricate web of her
hair holding the pillow in

Place he had the sweet taste
of her in his mustache was
listening to the sound of the

Breeze in a bottlebrush the
sigh of his heart morning
doves in the trees a little

Further out the muffled
roar of the 405 six or
eight lanes of metal

Boxes moving in each
direction rushing toward
the death of their dreams

MUSIC

red hair and black leather
my favorite color scheme

—Richard Thompson

I lower the lights
lie down on my bed and
rolled into the shadows
I see you—

—Arthur Rimbaud

Sierra Wind

Who could have known
it would whip your hair
to a frenzy provoking

Fantasies of what it
might be like to be
tangled there heat

From your eyes
shimmering across
the parking lot

What happened there
afterwards I never felt
the same not ever again

Rimbaud Stops At The Liquor Store In Mojave

The wind with so little
to hold its interest is
making speeches about

Her hair sky splattered
with clusters of vermillion
edged thunderheads the

Sound of drunken boats
filling the air and nothing
made much sense without her

Talkin' Cow-Calf Pairs At The Coney Island Bar

The bigger the hat

The smaller the ranch

January

Could be Butte
Battle Mountain
Livingston or

Lamoille it's all
about the same
in late January

Rust pitted pickups
bounce around
3:00 A.M. chuckholes

Passenger doors
swinging open wide

Honey, I'm sorry
would you please

Just get back
in the truck

Traffic

The longer you last
the less you care
—Marilyn Monroe

Why is it always late
Friday afternoon with
one of the four wheels

Of your heart going flat
you find someone behind
you wants to run up your ass

While up front someone
is braking in anticipation
of *it* actually breaking

Dilemma

The mistake always
trying to word it
too soon

The regret always
in not having
done it sooner

Thinking About Her Reading Creeley

Three hundred miles into
the midst of a Great Basin
night February thoughts

Of her red lips tumble
through his mind errors
accumulate like late snow

In a high desert ditch bank
building out of our sight
the terrible thoughts of time

What did I know thinking
myself able to go alone
all the way

The Ole Mind-Body Split Healed

She thinks about swaying to Joe Ely
he thinks Leonard Cohen's lyrics

When she suddenly turns to him
asks about the words to *Suzanne*

Again And Again

I've been thinking bout
nothing but you for two
straight days your voice

The memory the fire of
your touch becoming
fluent sounds the scroop

Of your skirt as you
descend the staircase
take me in your mouth

Becoming the liquid line
drawn by my tongue
through your delta sounds

So much like music sliding
into you that even the rain
bursts into flame

Gardening

January quickly
becomes July
around here

What you plants
comes in spades
or not at all

The Perennial's Lament

Spring fully sprung again
he finds himself talking
to this year's leaves about

Exactly the same things
he spoke of to last year's

Independence Day

Standing by the fence
listening to some low
down blues fireworks

Over Rattlesnake pale
fade in comparison to
the blaze of her pink

Dress glowing against the
oncoming obsidian night

Seven Come Eleven

He remembers Lew Welch's line
about muses and mistresses
about confusion about trouble

And he thought he knew what
Lew meant until the wind from
her hair rolled both his way

At The Mizpah

She stands naked
at the window skin
glowing from the bath

Pulls the lace curtain
over to one side pink
rain pulsed motel neon

Reflecting up from five
floors below dapples
her alabaster profile

In gray light she will
reach for him soon
she'll come across

The bed to his warmth
and with the breast of
Redlick Summit draped

In dark nimbus rain
turning to snow they'll
head north then west

Through the world's
longest deepest valley
peaks on either side

Stiff with late
spring snow

Medusa In Red Mountain

In the Mojave amidst
miles of solar collectors
a forest of windmills

He pulls over at the
rickety roadside inn
once a shabby brothel

Flypaper dangles on
the porch swamp cooler
groans against the heat

He steps into the musty
mildewed darkness with
acrid smoke hanging

In the air she sits legs
crossed leaning back
against the beer cooler

Cutoffs barely coming
to the top of her thigh
white against the black

Naugahyde with one
hand she lifts hair from
the back of her neck

Holds it on top of her
head a sinuous mass
of red vipers below

Which one dusty black
mule dangles from red
painted toes the other

Mule hooks the rung
of the stool moves to
Chet's elegiac trumpet

As she reaches back into
the cooler for a piece
of ice presses it against

Her neck the melt runs
down to faux white
pearl snaps on her tight

Black top she draws on
her cigarette blows the
smoke toward him looks

over and says *well well*
up till now been nothin' but
heat and wind round here

Desert Saudade

What seems to matter
most is how it matters
still how the wind can

Become the achingly
beautiful recognition
of a sad song's yearning

An end of the world
waltz through the slate
black great basin night

Where absence becomes
presence where we turned
lost temporarily what it

Was we thought we had
blinker suddenly on
right lane turning left

To nowhere ninety
miles out and
wondering why

Music

—A bar story for Valerie & Jack Fulton

Dave saved up his money
bought a bar he liked classical
music and since it was in the

Middle of the Great Basin
miles from the likelihood
to hear any such thing he

Decided what the hell called
it Mozart Club he really
couldn't remember whether

It was Chopin Satie Mozart
or Mendelssohn that moved
him so but he liked the sound

Of Mozart he painted a big
skeleton on the side of the
bar emblazoned with This Guy

Drank Water a lot of locals
thought it was pretty funny
began to call the watering hole

Home every month or so Dave
and his painter friend would
make the day-long supply run

To Reno they were at the Santa Fe
had consumed way too many
picons that great Friday night

Basque steak dinner were
standing at the bar drinking
Winnemucca coffees debating

Whether they should head back
or not and if they did who
given all the picons was most

Qualified to drive when she
walked in she was the most
drop-dead beautiful woman

Dave'd ever seen she could've
been Northern Italian English
Irish with a stunning mane of

Red hair and amazing legs
after a quick look around
she walked to the end of

The bar sat on a stool crossed
her legs high Dave and
everyone else in the bar was

Speechless she'd silenced
the rowdy Friday night
crowd just by walking

In like the way sometimes
the sun going down can
stop a wind that's been

Howling all day across
the desert's face Dave
watched his heart tumble

Out flop around on the bar
like some fish sensing it was
after all the seventh year

Of a drought and this just
might be it would you like
a drink he blurted out

Their eyes locked and that
was it they spent the next
three hours drinking at a

Small table in the back
Dave kept feeding her small
slices of lime from the palm

Of his hand and she'd laugh
oh how she'd laugh she'd
get up every so often and

Go make a phone call Dave
would watch her walk
to the pay phone and back

Wondering wondering he
even reached under the table
once squeezed her leg

Thinking oh my God what
a stupid thing to do now
she'll walk out I'll never

See her again but she stayed
and talked and drank they
both felt some kind of furnace

Burning like never before
until she finally said I have
to go my brother's coming

To pick me up she left
with her brother Dave left
with his painter friend they

All ended up standing in
the parking lot Dave and
her just staring at each other

Neither wanting to break
the connection Jeezus
Christ Dave the painter

Said put your goddamn
eyes back in your head
open the goddamn door

Who's to say what happened
next or how it happened but
Dave hung around Reno

Until he saw her again that's
all it took a done deal never
a question she came back

To the Mozart Club that's
when the music really began
from then on everyone kept

Commenting how amazing
it all was how right it all
seemed how good they

Looked together how glad
they were for Dave this is
it Dave thought at last he

Began to think of waltzing
toward the millennium
on a sea of melodious

Light but then there's
always life it goes on
as they say and it does

But it also can just suddenly
stop he went down to the bar
one day came home to find

Her gone no note no word
nothing her clothes her shoes
she was obsessive about her

Collection of black patent high
heels everything but her still
there Dave looked and looked

Went back up to Reno but
nothing not a trace no one
even knew her it was as if

She had never existed as if
it had all never happened
but Dave knew it had he

Tried to forget but couldn't
because he didn't really
want to he never did look

At another woman drank
more than a bit it was worse
than fighting the weather

All that thinking about it
wondering what had
happened why there were

All these years of nights they
might have been together
but weren't it was thirty years

Later almost to the day this
gorgeous redhead walked
into the Mozart Club

Everyone stumblin' over
themselves hittin' on her
trying to buy her a drink

Everyone but Dave who just
sat at the end of the bar
nursing his drink she wasn't

Interested in all the attention
only wanted one thing anyone
here named Dave she asked

Down there end of the bar
Dave's painter friend said
she walked to the end of

The bar everyone watching
every part of her move
Dave she asked yeah he

Said looking up from his
drink his bloodshot blues
meeting her amber ones

What'ya want I'm your
daughter she said and
so the story was told

How her mother was
from a very wealthy
Austrian family how

She came to the States
on holiday with her brother
how she'd walked into a bar

In Reno one Friday night and
fallen head-over-heels in love
with the piercing blue eyes

Of a guy named Dave who
owned a bar how her grand
mother had disowned her

Mother for having the
audacity to do that how
after that it didn't seem

To matter until her
grandmother fell ill
wanted her daughter

Back home before
she died how her
grandmother sent

Her son back to the States
to bring her daughter back
how after that her mother

Was in a car accident they
were able to save the baby
but not her how her grand

Mother recovered raised
her daughter's baby never
mentioned any of it how

Her uncle told her all about
it only after her grandmother
finally died

JUST PAST LABOR DAY

there is nothing to do
as the sun goes down
over the flat horizon

—Tom Clark

in a landscape where nothing
officially exists absolutely
anything may happen

—Reyner Banham

Rodeo's In Town

Gaggle of tanned cowgirl
poptarts a stunning array
the tightest Wranglers

Every conceivable color
you can imagine wiggling
their asses cooing to one

Another as they bend
over the mirrors at the
cosmetic counter in Raley's

Local Knowledge

Wyatt 'round

Nope

When's he comin'

Dunno

You're just
a fuckin' fountain
of information

Ain't you

Don't matter
what I say

It'll turn out
to be wrong

Erotic

The knowledge
the conviction
you are wanted

From there it's a
short step to going
too far enough

Fulcrum

Sure we can think about
it that way if you like we
can perhaps talk about

What it all means try to
define what we believe
what we want wonder

What or who is God
what or who will make
us happy ponder

Differences between
involvement and
commitment watch

Definitions change trans
mute into first one thing
then another wind whipped

Clouds a sudden burst
of sparrows from the
lilacs but now let's simply

Applaud the sight you
wiggling out of your
jeans turning toward

Me with the smile that
makes us both realize
the best thing about

Today is just that it
could become tomorrow
again and again finding

At last balancing
a promise with
what lasts

Nevada Weather

Changes so quickly
if you don't like it

You can either wait
fifteen minutes or

Look out another
window

Scenes From The French Revolution

How just exactly at sunset
sunset the two peacocks fly
up top of the telephone pole

Perch there as if to get one last
glimpse of the dying light briefly
the blaze of their iridescent blue

Breasts backlit by the rising
silver dollar moon almost
makes you forget how earlier

They were just two more
marauding peasants busily
ransacking your garden

Amor Fati

Always late never
early she thinks
she's both worth

Every painful
moment worth
less for causing it

Can see Tuesday
turn to Wednesday
without regret

And wants him
to forget she gives
him reason again

And again not to

Night Music

You don't notice at first
how it starts slowly
from far off the single

Plop plop of drops
on the last of fall's
leaves a slightly off

Key sonata moving
from cottonwood
to fledgling cherry

Over Russian olive
to where it must
really end suddenly

It's so quiet you forget
how it began listen
again and again for

The first telltale notes
moving toward you
small arpeggios from

The west yes it's late
but maybe never too
you tell yourself

Through the eerie
dissonance of
clustered chords

That her touch will
come again and
when it does even

The rain as it falls
will feel like it's
coming home

Morna

Somewhere out there this
month's pomegranate
incarnation of the moon

Rises above inflated
bouffant clouds
remembering the

Time years ago far
to the west how he
carried her how she

Pulled him toward
her gave her pause
for a moment just

Before it all came
rushing swirling
back so she felt

Around for her early
morning hastily kicked
off heels slipped into

Them and slowly
began to climb the sad
tattered obsidian stairs

Lure

Just what is it
what thing so
hooks my eye

The neon backlit
swollen web of
her amber hair

The rhythm
her heels beat
on the sidewalk

Or is it a glimpse
just the glimpse
briefly through

The slit skirt
the tops of her
black stockings

That snags my
mind pulls it
toward a sense

Other than common
filled with thoughts
of just what might be

Cellaring

He once thought of her
as the wine you put
away when company

Comes hints of a great
body nicely finished
even now in the musty

Breath of late autumn
what there was left
remained distinct a blood

Red vintage of its own
which he drank
to her memory or not

Sisyphus And The Albatross

He often felt cast in
a little known Beckett
play where alone out

On a country road
under a tree in the
evening he'd find

A box bearing the slain
bird of good omen and
he'd spend all night

Most of the next day
pushing the rotten
carcass first here

Then there then here
and back there until
late in the afternoon

When he'd give up
bury it fall asleep
when he woke later

That evening the box
was back and he began
pushing every evening

It was the same push
it here push it there
bury it fall asleep and

Awake to the box
I can't go on
I'll go on

Poetry Readings Dim Bulbs And Bad Renditions Of Chamber Music

Although it has been said
that you can get through
anything if you know it's

Going to end sometimes
in the midst of it all it
begins to seem that it

Will never change never
end never the longer it lasts
the longer they drone on

And on and on the less
you seem to care

Just Past Labor Day

Sleep will become
a language spoken
only in a distant

Country where the air
stills suddenly chills
the penumbral hours

Before dawn memories
of August's passionate
heat recede while the

Silent evasive demon
of doubt begins to
show you how water

Can enter stone fracture
the heart of the matter

SHOES

a fetish is a story masquerading as an object

—Robert Stoller

the best thing about a high heel is that
it's like putting your ass on a pedestal

—Veronica Webb

A Florentine Affair

Last seen under black
spaghetti strap sheath
in the Palazzo Vecchio

Neither sure what it
was shadows perhaps
heels on moonlit cobble

Stones memories a
room high in the Alps
her hand on his face

That caused her to come
completely undone hair
cascading from its clasp

Falling in anticipation

On The Veranda

Bare minimal four inch
summer strappy heels
revealing and concealing

Amid clink of flutes
on afternoon veranda
the straps binding her

Red painted toes made her
feel Leonard forbidding
delivery deep inside he

Heard scroop of pleated
skirt heels clicking staccato
on tiles smell of jasmine

On the wind in her hair

Velvet Drapes

Hint of Victoriana
eyelets laces up to
her knees pointiest

Toes sleek slender heels
often prompted people
to say my grandmother

Had shoes like that truth
be told they take too
damn long to undo when

Rushed arriving a little
too early for tea gramma
would be shocked to see

Her head thrown back into
velvet drapes skirt hiked up
her legs those boots locked

Tightly around him

High Heels Wet Streets

After he watched
the tantalizingly
slow strip she

Shimmied into long
slit black skirt black
fox hat knee high

Tight on the calf
stiletto numbers
and pulling boots

Up skirt down she
plunged headlong
into the cloudburst

Drenched night in
search of an uptown
cab without even

Thinking about an umbrella

Fifty Seventh And Sixth

Three A.M. extreme yet
shrewd just five inch
pumps bra garter belt

And bas de soie noire
from Agent Provocateur
under fur coat a little

Tipsy on a deep into
December late night
her hair splashed

Across a pillow on
the forty first floor
window full of snow

Falling in gray dawn
light her shoes in the
air just watching

The look on his face

Black And White

A sucker for ankle straps
made her want to be
pinned up ala Bettie Page

Those other gorgeous '40s
noir film queens with
backlit Veronica Lake

Hair smoke curling from
red even in black-and-white
lips that smirk just hinting

At her dominant side

Dressage

Though not meant
for stable these
seemed to inspire

A rhapsody of queries
invitations is she going
riding would she *like*

To go riding and it
wasn't horses although
a little riding crop

Worked well on both

Wild Pair

Folklore told her to be
careful you might see
panties in the reflection

So she didn't wear any
nor look for redeeming
social qualities with these

Sleek no-nonsense patent
thrillers which went well
with leather garter belt

Made her want to be taken
from behind just so they
could watch the gleaming

There beneath them

Neon Martini

Eye catching
illusion illicit
'50s Hollywood

Glamour bright
painted cadmium
nails glowing neon

Martini glasses
Marilyn teetering
along in feather boa

Tight black skirt
binding as she
stoops to retrieve

A dropped earring
nothing at all could
hold her back from

Her less than discreet
tightly laced corselet
thigh highed stiletto

Roadhouse liaison

Frisson

Lycra dress short as
spike heels were tall
under floor length

Leather coat she
noticed they were
louder than any

Other pair could
silence the most
conversation laden

Room made her feel
like she was stalking
her prey and that

Was simply thrilling

Whispers

A quiet aura louche
yet reserved suggesting
possibilities when she

Crosses her legs he
hears swish of sheer jet
black stockings tied by

Elegant asymmetrical
black velvet straps under
the table whispering

High but not too high

Car To Bar

Do me do me now
the tallest pair of all
whispers from car to bar

In tight leather mini over
lace gartered fishnets she's
the wicked dream witch

Best nightmare come true
takes no prisoners heels
puncture head and heart

Most of everything else

OLD ANGEL MIDNIGHT

a toss of the dice will never abolish chance

—Stéphane Mallarmé

I was wondering how far to go…what's
the point where it becomes dangerous
to go any further…the point of wondering
comes when you think you've gone too far

—Sam Shepard

Blue Moon

It's a bad moon the radio says
a blue moon with haste and
horses things begin to whirl

Out of control the mercury
keeps rising but life goes on
like in a ball of snakes you try

To follow one body but
no matter how long you
watch you just can't do it

Idiot Wind

Blows incessantly through
false spring early April days
battering thoughts what if

What then back and forth
making it impossible to get
water where you want it

Things tumble together
a whirlwind of confusion
he'd sorted it down

To what really matters but
questions if what he thinks
matters really does and if so

How can this idiot wind
rend it so completely
yesterday's tent torn

Asunder everything he
thought dear sailing away

Heisenberg On The Fourth Of July

Are you he asks
what do you
mean she replies

Knowing is a feeling
something happening
or about to happen

No she says you
don't really think
so or do you

Not thinking
but knowing
feeling small

Breakages as they
occur he knows
uncertainty not

As a principle
but as occurrence
as virga rain

That falls without
touching the ground

Augury

New year's eve almost
a new year artificially
endowed epiphany in

The ceaseless flow of time
ritual perhaps from a dim
paleolithic past where we

Banked the fire higher
against the storm dreamed
of returning home again

The rain came in satin
sheets spilling off the
umbrella back in the room

We lean into one another
listen to the deluge all
around us streams rivers

Are swollen rushing over
their banks here we are
dry warm wrapped up

Together in the eye of this
hundred year storm and
while there will surely

Be trouble downstream
we think we've divined
some means of washing

The flotsam and jetsam
from our lives if only
for this night

Dead Reckoning

Plans topple are cast aside
senses other than common
lured by arousal find stasis

In sweetness that might last
the spark of speech arches
out from its narrow path

Connecting oh so many dots
out here on the edge of the
map the way is in the going

Seeing one thing as another
at the edge of the light we cut
through the bullshit journey

Side by side try to elegantly
hold back the night by
realizing what matters most

Apparition

Frozen in the glow
of your headlights
hovering in pogonip

Above the ditchbank
something you never
thought you'd see but

All at once there it is
her shimmering face
saying come on this

Way glowing there
for just a second then
just as quickly gone

Baking

She was in the kitchen
baking a preternaturally
warm spring night small

Rivulets of sweat ran down
her neck between her breasts
he was out smoking under

Thunderheads a rising full
moon wondering why certain
things happened watching

Her through the window
timer was set bread had
begun to rise she tucked

Stray strands of auburn hair
back behind her ear licked
her finger leaned back against

The counter as a sudden
cloudburst sent him
hurtling through the door

Bon Appétit

She remembered that
time beside the Seine
and the taste of paté

She began to think
of geese raising them
just for their livers

She remembered how
it felt drifting toward
Morpheus afterward

She liked to remember
often thought of him
the taste of raspberries

On her lips and every
time she did she was
suddenly hungry

Nvr Say Nvr

There was no moon yet
the light of only one star
when he saw her sitting

There thinking just what
it was that he was but it
was later that he heard

Her clearly very clearly
yet without speaking
say it was all too fast

Too much but do not
go do not stop not now

Plum

In green silk against
Italian modernist
plum décor patent

Pumps quickly kicked
off hair spread wide
across black sheets he'd

Never been that close
to anything like this
was now considering

The possibilities of
putting out the
fire with gasoline

Climate Change

Breeze from your hair
takes my breath sparks
arc across the room all

The lights in town dim
then wink out sheets of
ice drip slivers of light

To the floor your eyes
are moist we're standing
in a warm lake it begins

To boil steam rises
condenses on the tiles of
chambers long forgotten

Far away the level
of a distant ocean
rises a full three feet

Fall Bulbs

The unexpectedly easy surprise
that slides suddenly into her
springtime eyes as legions of
priapic gladioli alliums and
narcissi oh so willingly rise

Murmur

In the corner booth after blood
dark merlot grilled porterhouse
she turns the ice cream spoon

Over on her tongue suddenly
so quiet just the murmur of
her diaphanous legs long silver

Earrings brushing her neck
thoughts of what might be
echoing off red brick walls

Pigeons

He remembered her asking
what d'ya think as from a sea
of black leather a rising

Exaltation of pigeons
plunged headlong into
a tattered azure sky

Glitter

From across the half darkened room
she speaks of *Lady Chatterley's Lover*
touches herself in the secret mirror

Of how she suddenly feels moving
shamelessly she crosses uncrosses her
legs revealing then concealing all of

Winter's glitter on the midnight tree

Old Angel Midnight

Glimpsed through black
tulle of the screen door

Moon's pale crescent flesh
ringed in an amber peplum

Drifting along on eerie silk

DISPATCHES

one's destination is never a place
but a new way of seeing things

—Henry Miller

the poem is always in your
hometown but you have a better
chance of finding it another

—Richard Hugo

Multi-Culturalism

Trembling twilit climb
to thirty-five thousand
feet above the Atlantic

Hurtling toward Zurich
orthodox Jews Muslim
women leather pants

Pointy spike-heeled
patent boots California
cabernet travel agents

Shepherding flocks
from the Jersey shore
toward Prague

Driving In France

The plane trees
arbes d'alignment
lining both sides

Of most roads in
France numbered
more than three

Million at the end
of the nineteenth
century now thanks

To cars veering off
the road there are only
two hundred thousand

Chartres

The spire soaring
above mid-winter
fields pulls the rented

Opel toward it with
an intensity similar
to the faithful who

In 1145 began to
imagine the gothic
shape of God today

It's so cold my nose
freezes to the camera

Thomery

Sick with a fever
delirious wanting
just to be squished

Like a postage stamp
all night long the black
wind stripped branches

Danced across the wall
above the bed moving
to call and response

Steady pulse of the Seine
squeal of Paris express
au revoir au revoir she

Says in first gray light
demain perhaps *demain*

At The Louvre

Russians motion me over
to their black Mercedes

Offer a trunk full of
guns furs cigarettes

White Heat

In the darkened third
floor flat sur la rive
gauche just a glass of

Vin rouge the brilliant
white light from the
inside of her thighs

Above the welts
of black stockings

Pere Lachaise

The largest cemetery
in Paris all the famous
dead and gone signposts

To find each and every
one save Jim Morrison
whose signs are either

Defaced or gone his grave
covered with light my fire
and show me the way to

Next whiskey bar graffiti
bouquets of dead flowers
wine bottles skirts high

Heels scribbled poems
offerings cigarettes
beer cans and joints

Le Jour De L'an

Last night balconies
of the Palais de Chaillot

Filled with champagne
and firecrackers all

Of Paris on the metro
to watch the digital clock

Slide toward a century
with three zeros

Saint-Émilion

If anything new is
put up it must be
made to look old

Saint Valerie was
beheaded for her
faith but picked

Up her own head
and walked
now she's said

To watch over
the wine and
vineyards

While Ursuline
nuns sell the
same macaroons

They've made
since 1100
just another

Incandescent
loop in the
history of things

Amsterdam

Canals three meters
deep local folklore
suggests one meter

Is sludge another dis
carded or dumped
bicycles

Keizersgracht

Guy across the way
third floor book-lined
flat licks an envelope

Under green reading
light takes off his
glasses rubs his brow

Sips some wine looks
across the canal the
sound of leather heels

Aimless drunken chatter
on cobblestones below
will go on all night long

A tall disheveled blonde
appears behind him
rubs his neck then his

Shoulders he nods licks
another envelope drinks
a little more wine reaches

Out to her turns off the light
as a thumbnail moon rises
in clear below zero air by

Morning hotel maids cannot
make it to work all the ducks
are frozen solid in the canals

Driving In Italy

Lost in the rain trying
to find the road to Milan
at the crossroads three

Signs Milan to the left
Milan to the right and
Milan straight ahead

Turning left one half
hour later we're back
at the crossroads

Turning right back again
but straight ahead puts us
directly on the autostrada

Triesenberg

A long day driving
fog so dense can
barely see up the

Twisting switchback
lift from carpark opens
opens onto mist shrouded

Dripping wet courtyard
feels as if we've been
yanked back four hundred

Years the room's veranda
overlooks the entire country
snow crawls down the Alps

Mendelssohn's violin
concerto begins on
Radio Suisse mixing

With spooky sounds of
giant cowbells drifting
up through the mist

Istanbul

It's raining New Year's
Eve too dervishes whirl
in Sirkeci Station gulls

Circle the Hagia Sofia
taxis scuttle on slick
cobblestones dodge

Rug merchants in the
café at the crossroads
of east and west head

Scarves bright floral
shawls stiletto boots

Dolmabahçe

Kemal Ataturk founder
of modern Turkey
routed the Ottomans

Abolished the fez and
polygamy built the first
brewery died in a room

Here the bed covered
with the crescent moon
and single star of the

Turkish flag all the
clocks in the palace
are stopped at 9:05

The minute he died

Talking With A Waiter In The Azores

—Faja Grande, Flores

Out here in the middle
of the Atlantic where
Europe ends we're told

It has been cooking for
days but is done now

Will the restaurant
be open tomorrow

Maybe yes

Maybe no

It depends if there
are enough people

Who want to eat

Driving In The Spanish Basque Country

Jose Marie in Zarautz
warns that since we
have French license

Plates we'd best be
careful or they will
flat our tires

Bilbao

Guggenheim same color
as the horizontal sheets
of relentless rain we

Duck down Calle Kalera
for chipirónes en su tinta
squid cooked in its own

Ink a steaming white
bowl of salty blacknes

Bilbao

Guggenheim same color
as the horizontal sheets
of relentless rain we

Duck down Calle Kalera
for chipirónes en su tinta
squid cooked in its own

Ink a steaming white
bowl of salty blackness

At The Prado

The swell of hip below
her bustier nipped waist
reminded him of plunging

Into the narrowing canyon
of a Nevada two-lane

Zestoa

ETA graffiti splatters
the walls we park
along with everyone

Else in front of the
many no parking
signs drink vino

Tinto talk with fellow
pilgrims from Navarre
Zaragoza and beyond

Waiting to see the cave
paintings at Ekain which
must rest awhile so they

Will not be destroyed by
our breath finally we go
up the steep muddy trail

To the caves the way lit
only by a few flashlights
animals follow contours

Of the cave walls hands
waved in the beams of
light cause the paintings

To move across the rocks
much as they must have
in paleolithic firelight

Horses bison salmon goats
bears even the mother and
father of Bambi a Basque

To Spanish to French to
English translation of the
forgotten word for deer

Santiago De Compostela

Cathedral built on the spot
where remains of St. James
or at least a finger or toenail

Mysteriously appeared here
after he was beheaded in the
holy lands for more than a

Thousand years the faithful
have walked here at the end
of the road we attend the

Pilgrim's mass the woman
next to us talking a mile
a minute about the goings

On fanning herself as if
there would be no end
to it the botafumerio

The world's largest censer
is filled with wood and
incense hoisted aloft by

Eight robed monks and
swung back and forth
showering the pilgrims

With embers and ash
afterward we join the
line to troop behind

The altar up the stairs
dished from so many
feet for so many years

To rub the similarly
dished head of the saint
himself then back into

Town for bowls of padron
peppers in olive oil and
salt unos pican otros no

Oostende

Arriving late we miss
the hydrofoil have
to take the ferry

Brits ending their
weekend holiday
stack cases of beer

Five or six high
on the small tables
drink it all before

Landing at Dover

Mind The Gap

Gap between centuries
how peoples from an
empire where the sun

Once never set have
now colonized London
Thames as ravine between

St. Paul's Cathedral and
Tate Modern's re-purposed
power station gap between

Classes the royals and
the rest of us chasm
between what we feel

How we act Emma Clarke's
computer enhanced voice
in Victoria Station robotic

Yet seductive warning us
of the space between
platform and train

Looking At Photographs In London

Posing and posturing on
the verge of adolescence
the Polish girl trying to

Figure out what to do
with her limbs the orange
bikini-ed American from

Hilton Head seemingly
ready for a go at just
about anything

At Sir John Soane's

Nurnies and hoohas
from across the centuries
seti and sarcophagi

Plundered from here
and there a dazzling
array of cluttered nooks

Impossible to link
any one thing with
any other just

The sheer revelry
of them all here
together

Belfast

A couple pints in a snug at
the Crown Liquor Saloon
where you can sip unseen

Where revolutionary
conspiracies clandestine
meetings once took place

Probably still do dinner
at nouvelle Moroccan place
the cute art student waitress

Suggests we go see murals
from the troubles you oughta
go she says but be careful

Don't take sides keep your
mouth shut take a black cab
though it's a bit pricey two

Neighborhoods Shankill Road
protestant Falls Road catholic
run parallel out of central Belfast

A wall separates them thirty
feet high wrapped in concertina
wire gardens planted right up

To it on both sides the theory
being if you're gonna cause
some trouble you won't be

Able to skip back into your
neighborhood would have
to go all the way down to

Town center work your way
back up the long winding
road home after seeing

The murals we pass the police
station windowless fortified
gun-laden sitting over the

Barrier solid steel gate slammed
shut each day at dusk the cabbie
says murals like pubs have

Become simply part of the
culture for both sides you just
do what you can he says

He's going to Turkey or
perhaps Barcelona on holiday
whichever is warmer

Belfast To London

Two young women
on the train raincoats
short pleated skirts

Some seriously tall
shoes chattering about
eros and thanatos

Each with a copy
of *On the Road*
talking about Kerouac

How much he matters
all the rest they
say is hogwash

Dublin

A traveling professional
woman with the most
amazing eye makeup

Tells us that since she's
Irish she does what she
can looks forward to

Holiday and batting
her eyes over a plate
of kippers wants to

Know how we're doing
after you know *our*
trouble in New York

Driving In Scotland

Hard to get used to
being on the other
side of the road

But in the highlands
it's nothing compared
to their habit of passing

On blind curves they
take it as a sport call
it reckless overtaking

Camster

After the snowstorm
we'd driven way north
of Inverness to see the

Carirns with Norway
floating out there on
the horizon nothing

Grew but heather so
purple it was black
the wooden walkway

Across the bog glazed
with ice the sign saying
don't even think about

Stepping off here the
mound of stacked black
stones cold slick reminder

Of the realities of life in
the neolithic highlands
no one there but us and

Some soggy sheep next day
at breakfast after telling
the doctor from Nairn of

Our adventure he nods says
why would'ya go up there
'tis a bit bleak don't ya think

Bobby Burns Night
Glasgow

Rain turning to thick
heavy slush even the
architecture slumps

Under sheer weight
of cold damp air the
Miss Bobbie Burns

Contest on the radio
promises very short
kilts very tall booties

A winner that will be
apokin' the haggis

Edinburgh

Our cabbie's company
is named Dogs of War
like most men in

Scotland he's got
a buzz cut when
asked why he says

Well we are Scot so
it's a might thrifty
but if you ever get

Into a bit of a tussle 'tis
not much to grab onto

HOW THE LIGHT GETS IN

the ponies run the girls are young
the odds are there to beat
you win a while and then it's done
your little winning streak

—Leonard Cohen

tell the Truth but tell it Slant

—Emily Dickinson

Solstice

Solstice the longest night
we watch stars become
words to light the dark

Hours revealing how the
heart again and again
infuses hope with desire

Jigsaw

Traces of snowmelt
at sidewalk's edge

Sky clearing ice by
morning nothing

Really matches or
lines up in any way

All that's left is just
treacherous edges

Buds

Almost half moon
up early before
the sun leaves

Three honkers fly
by heading west
air so still

You can hear
buds on the lilac
pop open

Old Movies

The accumulation of
things as miscellany
projected clear across

The room frame after
frame dissolving in
the film's grain what

Was once clear loses
focus blurs the rustle
of fabric whisper of

Nylon as she walks
by without noticing
him watching her

Long Distance

Driving along the coast
road two lane seems
like summer but it's

Cold fog shrouded
we're passing cars
too old to be driven

Anywhere by anyone
when the phone
starts ringing

Bridges

You hang what you
cannot say out to dry
with the laundry try

To surmise correctly
from incomplete
information think

About bridges delicate
tendrils to cross over
natural obstacles sighs

Whispers exclamations
a shadowed smile
touch of a hand how

They allow us to cross
over span what we
thought we couldn't

You come over to me
I drive back into you a
journey worth repeating

One that might be better
than it's already been

It Might Be A Fer Piece

Don't know where
the hell we are

But we're makin'
good time

Come To Winnemucca

—found at the Star Broiler

Having taken a few
too many at a hotel
dance a pretty young

Thing ran outside fell
over a trash barrel
where this guy saw

Her picked her up
carried her to his room
next morning he wired

His partner close office
sell everything come
to Winnemucca they

Throw away better
stuff here than you
can buy in California

Cornell

Looking into a sealed world
a cosmology of fragments
choreographed junk vortex

Of horror vacui past and
present on patrol along
the horizon of dread

Weighing just what goes
where the amount of
pressure necessary for

Cast offs remnants to be
combined the melancholy
of snow in the distance

White on the Stillwaters
like stars on the road
of the dead the sun's

Yellow rays are running
out of heat a fountain of
sand begins to sing in the

Mountains bits of cottonwood
suggest water might be near
but light on water is different

Than oil on water the wind
stirs the sage and leafless
willow dust devils dance

In the distance the black
stone is broken and over
in the corner the moon

Struggles up this surely
must be the place
where crying begins

Paradigm Shift

Struggling through an
afternoon de Kooning
splatters the sky's edge

With a huge brush
stroke of red along the
western rim but not

Enough to last soon
the moon comes round
all dolled up in silver lamé

Odd Dreams

So much to do under this
tremulous sky hard to see
what might come by through

All the smoke from distant
fires endless re-runs on TV
the county fair is now a

Country fair load the empty
glasses and salsa stained
plates into the dishwasher

Power bumps off by Bic
lighters the search for
candles begins cats romp

To and fro hurl themselves
down the hall odd dreams
recurrent schemes blacked

Out thoughts grabbing what
he can he looks here and
then there but still can't find

A tomato that tastes like
a tomato and so on he
goes as he ever went

Code

Small figures appear
to be dancing in the
distance out of focus

How such things can
count for so much
is some kind of code

A random intensity
that appears then rides
away on the wind

Miles To Go

The moon fills the murky
frozen ditch water with
odd trembling light beside

Coils of rusting barbed wire
rabbitbrush stacks of old tires
there were still many miles

To go on iced over roads
so cold the snow crunches
like walking on bubblewrap

Virga And Zephyr

Elmore's talkin' bout
the sky's tears it's so
hot not many will

Make it spot the dust
for very long sudden
wind whispers about

Tonight's full moon
saying *take her there*

Glimpse

She stoops to
pick up her shoes

A quick glimpse
of stocking tops

The sound of snow
falling quietly

Among the trees

Femme Noire

Femme as woman
ruche as hive of activity
pleated folded together

Fatale not as fatal but
inevitable dry ache
of absence longing

The stuff of fado on
a noire night like this
oracles say the idle

Pleasures of these days
cannot be guaranteed
time becomes malleable

Morning slips by
unnoticed afternoon
clouds up power

Bumps sudden
cumulonimbus threaten
darkness rushes in to

Fill the void for the
nonce the moon that
was not here rhymed

Perfectly with vermouth
stain of her sweet red lips
on the rim of everything

Heading East

Blood stained fleece
in the rearview

Carson Sink full
even in January

Lovelock
heart of Nevada

Melody
doing cocktails

At the Martin
in Winnemucca

Loretta waiting
by the mailbox

In her four-wheel
with dualies

Thirty-five miles
out of Battle Mountain

Lunatic Heart

so little we know of pleasure
—Kenneth Patchen

Awash in roses and
thrift store dreams
she sashays her mini

Skirt across the Scott's
Shady Court parking
lot ignoring crushed

Beer cans pot holes and
swinging around past
the empty tawdry pool

She lights a cigarette
drifts along with the
sound of her heels

On the concrete the
jukebox rhythm of
her lunatic heart

Springtime In Nevada

What elsewhere is brilliant
bunched spring grass bright
new after a rain green leaves

Or riot of fields awash in
bluebonnets here it's a brief
verdant blush on brown hills

The sage even the remnants
of a tumbled in roadhouse
cluster of rusting singlewides

Desertscape

Not so much color but its
absence dominated now
and then by a sudden burst

Of the not usual a red neon
sign way off in the distance
with no moon the smell of

Sage and tobacco smoke
suspended in sub-zero air

Armed Forces Day Parade
Hawthorne Nevada

More than four
hours long

Over a hundred
eighty entries

Horses and Harleys
in equal number

Every boy over twelve
with a Coors Light

Every girl over twelve
with a baby

Somewhere Like Denio

Threadbare seen
better days motel
cracked asphalt

Parking lot swamp
cooler straining
against the heat

Lipstick stained
paper napkins
go cups crushed

Cigarette packs
dirty stock trucks
sound of sudden

Rain splattering on
dusty windshields

Bad Night

He could remember
the exact shape
it took the glare

On asphalt when
she dumped the
mop bucket how

It gleamed ran
toward him
like blood in

The parking lot
light now if he
could only

Remember what
in the fuck he did
with the car keys

Oh Well

What long time
Nevadans say
when given

Lemons
from which

Lemonade
cannot be made

Delight

She was walking past
drinking in the window's
reflection when he knew

For sure that delight was
a risk that her music will
persist its lovely sounds

Enabling us to hear the
spaces of silence amidst
the clicking of her heels

Boom And Bust

A cycle the state
has seen many
times which

Thelma Ritter
once described
as a place where

Anything goes
but also noted
we should not

Be surprised
when it got up
and went

Late Night Jazz

Stopped at a traffic light
clouds rumbling above
why is it trouble smells

Like rain in the desert
dust in the city only
a short ride from here

To there even the weather
listening to saxophones
from another era

Mesostic For Cage At 100

Just
abOut
anytHing except
four miNutes

thirty three seConds
And no more
miGht be
Enough

Punctuated Equilibrium

Haircut today gray
and black scattered
clouds across

Haphazard barbershop
linoleum not gradual
at all but you seem to

Notice it suddenly
all at once

Relativity

What my mother
called wormholes
in moth damaged

Sweaters Einstein
saw as openings
in space between

Parallel universes
where the apparent
distance between

Two things could
be shortened by
being further apart

Assuming of course
the contiguous distance
between them is solely

A matter of geography

Geography

In Missoula Paradise
is just seventy nine
miles from Hellgate

While in Vegas
it runs parallel
to the Strip

Sirius Moon

Incredibly still so hot
even the hay grows
impatient waiting

To be picked up
the moon appears
perky celestial nipple

Through lacey clouds
playing the old reveal
and conceal shell game

The only sound rising
then falling across the
lunar washed fields

Is the crickets bows
and fiddles playing the
sad old country refrain

Either it is
or it isn't

Again
and again
and again

Crown Of Bohemia

Her call comes from far
further west she says it
is raining so hard even

Her panties are soaked
some thirty hours later
thunder after mumbling

Around the sky like a
grumpy old man with
a broken toe finally lets

Loose and it begins here
too slowly at first but
builds to cloudburst

Afterward he finds the
heirloom hibiscus
basking in the touch

Of unexpected moisture
swelling toward bloom

All Hallows Eve

Beggars' night Yellow Springs
street corner trees all tarted
up in a profusion of colors

Tattered remnants of summer's
sleek green tresses now a skein
of rain slick dappled sequins

Alabaster moon on frigid black
nylon over bright red tipped
branches swaying in the wind

Tick Tock

Late night
reading in the
chilled window

Wind howling
outside chimes
begin clock says

0:00 time to
begin again

Three Below

Half-in half-out
under the eaves
lilacs drip crystalline

Stilettos three below
falling fast the moon
a hammered coin of

Light have you ever
thought about
holding ever held

Liquid possibility
in your hands felt
it harden into melody

These Days

Having too long
tried to make
sense of it all

To make it fit
contours of line
or mind only to

Realize all of it
even what he covets
most is evanescent

Flames dancing
walking the line
between real time

And the sublime

Deadheads

Going to pick up a donation
of deadheads in a weary dust
filled singlewide on a sandhill

A dozen miles off the highway
on a dirt track piled in a small
room the moose the bighorn

The antelope elk and all those
flies buzzing on the screenless
window looking for a way out

Made him think about those
whose past is unchanged
whose future is unknown

Whose heads increase in
value with death and he
started to wonder what life

Must be like under a clear
blue cloudless decapitated sky
that's less than an inch high

Ashes

Dirt is where the dreams must end
—James Welch

My mother was a tough
old broad a survivor my
sister says of it all polio

Bad husbands a good one
nine decades of changing
times in So-Cal no one

Wanted a big ceremony
nor knew what best to do
with her ashes kept them

For three years till mother's
day and since she'd always
liked flowers spread them in

The dirt beds on either side
of the front door the moon
was between the trees the

Wind in the leaves for days
afterward a fine powdered
dust clung to my levis

Popcorn

Microburst sends cats scuttling
to the rafters peacocks hustling
into leeward bushes after it

Passes we sit amid the turmoil
of blown down branches sip
cool drinks as thick rain drops

Spot her black camisole wind
blown catalpa blossoms tumble
like popcorn into her hair

Finally

When metaphor stops
becoming what it
might be and just is

Twists

Lemon wedge on espresso
sky footlighted by ballpark
screams for the home team

Everyone's talking about
the election one hand of
the clock says it matters

The other why bother
the weather is not so
much about what we

Know but how we feel
about all the little twists

Triple Digits

Rocks dust sagebrush
under a thirsty sky
the sun is so heavy

In August there is
loss triple digit heat
all around us while

The moon shines on
whatever it wants but
here its harsh light is

Muted by the arrival
on a breeze of sudden
rain her persistent mystery

All these years so striking
in her sumptuous chemise

Antiquities

The art historian saw
herself as vividly
contemporary equally

At home with the po-mo
decon boys and femmo
babble counterspeak but

Lately she'd been intrigued
with antiquities found
herself slipping into

Museums leaving at first
just fingerprints then bold
vermillion lipstick traces

Behind like cherries on the
hard snow white alabaster
of Grecian glutei maximi

The Nickel

Tonight the moon's
misshapen the nickel
he so carefully placed

On the tracks then
hunted for after
the train plunged

Into the tunnel hoping
wishing it into a bigger
more important thing

The kind of kiss that
kisses him back
saying yes

Spackling

Some things you can't
quite paint over the fist
through the wall hard

Bent air the season
never ending wakes
or loss for no reason

Just past midnight
star speckled Nevada
darkness at the signal

Corner of yes and no
jail on your left
movies on the right

The way out of here
toward what we ought
to be is the way home

WORK

Working on a book
he turns the page then
another and another

Through the hot dog
days of August
others who out

There in the sun
drive Cats move
dirt drive hammer

Into nail drop by
afterward hand
him a beer say

You call *that* work

Digital Dilemmas

The most frequently
accessed response

Has become the truest
and if it's so desirable

For things to happen
in real time what the

Hell might happen
in unreal time

Measuring

It's now more important
to measure time rather
than distance the second

Replacing foot and meter
but he had to decide
whether bridges were

Triumphs over physical
obstacles whether the
horizon was still a

Stress line whether
if he knew memories
would be all that

Was left would he
have remembered
better

Colors

Today the colors
are what they are
blue is sky brown dirt

Bees hum in the lilac
hot fields of hay wind
makes the trees visible

As they wave goodbye
to stillness her sleek
calves crossed just so

While the light leaves
every evening
right on schedule

Yard Sale

April's barely budded
trees fracture light
send it scuttling across

Dappled wood floors
while out the window
down the street on the

Edge of what we know
and rows of foreclosed
tract houses he watches

People walk to and fro
pulled back and forth
on invisible strings

A yard sale tableaux
things no one wants
spread on card tables

Man in green coveralls
another in red shirt
with an old camera

Kids playing with
mannequin parts
farther out still on

The outskirts of town
something supposedly
important is being said

While others carry all they
own around in tattered
black plastic garbage bags

How The Light Gets In

there is a crack in everything
that's how the light gets in
—Leonard Cohen

The moon inches up over
peaks to the east crawls
through the trees light

Leaking through cracks
between the leaves
crickets ring but soon

Their song will be done
coyotes begin to howl as
he wonders how these

Cracked and broken
windows manage to
hold onto the light

On even the darkest
streets of small desert
towns moon climbs

Higher above the trees
until he can see cracks
in the sidewalk in the

Way things are going
but bells still light up
when the music plays

Light's in the refrigerator
when he opens the door
in the bottle when he

Pulls the cork pours
her wine in the breeze
when he hears that song

And now in the stars
which are pinholes in
her ink black stocking

A run from the contrail of
an eastbound 747 snaking
its way around her thigh

About the Author

Poet, essayist, editor, publisher and artist, Kirk Robertson, has published more than twenty collections of poetry and his work has appeared in numerous magazines, journals and anthologies. His work is the recipient of several awards including the Wormwood Award for the Most Overlooked Book of Note and the Breakthrough Award from Watermark Press. In 1981, He received the Governor's Arts Award for Excellence in the Arts and was elected to the Nevada Writer's Hall of Fame in 1994. He has also written widely on the visual arts and a collection of essays on art and artists is in preparation. He lives in Fallon, Nevada where he is Program Director for the Churchill Arts Council.

Colophon

Designed and produced by Robert Blesse at the Black Rock Press, Department of Art, School of the Arts, University of Nevada, Reno. The typeface is Palatino, designed by Hermann Zapf for Linotype in 1948. Printed by BookMobile in Minneapolis